Erks Eye Vi

Memories of R.A.F. National Service

Front Cover Photo: "R.A.F. Station Gate Guardian – somewhere in England."

Erks Eye View

Memories of R.A.F. National Service

BREWIN BOOKS

First published in 1994 by
Brewin Books, Studley, Warwickshire, B80 7LG

ISBN 1 85858 054 4

British Library Cataloguing in Publication Data
A Catalogue record for this book is available from the British Library

Typeset by Avon Dataset Ltd, The Studio, Bidford on Avon, B50 4JH
Printed in Great Britain by The Cromwell Press, Broughton Gifford, Melksham, Wiltshire.

About the author

Eric William Russell was born in Small Heath, Birmingham in the early 1930s. He lived in the area throughout the blitz of the 1940s receiving his education at various local schools. An education which was completed by attending a two year engineering course at Bordesley Green junior technical school. It was but a short distance from the school to his first employment as a motor engineering apprentice at the Adderley Park factory of Morris Commercial Cars Ltd. At that time one of the principal manufacturers of light commercial vehicles in the UK. Over the next twenty years he had many different jobs within the company, such as fitter/mechanic in the vehicle experimental shop, service engineer, fleet engineer and finally as senior foreman of the transport department. The service at Morris was broken for a period of two years for national service.

He next joined Hills Diecastings (the diecasting division of Chrysler UK) for a very happy and informative five years as transport and stores superintendent.

The next and final career move was out of the motor industry to the distribution side of a major High St retail chain who operated in the region of one thousand stores throughout the UK. He remained with this company until ill health forced his early retirement from post of group transport manager in 1989.

He is a family man who at times is overwhelmed by female company, in the form of his wife, two daughters and five granddaughters.

He now lives with his wife in their retirement home, 1000 feet above sea level on the side of Titterstone Clee Hill in Shropshire, the county of his ancestors.

He is able to enjoy the views of over thirty miles from his window, live the life of a 'retired gentleman' in his much loved English countryside and indulge in the pleasant pastime of writing coupled with the study of genealogy.

Truly, a contented man.

PROLOGUE

The need for National Service in the 1950s was an extension of the necessity that had come about as a result of the Second World War. Following the war, the World, particularly Europe and Asia was in political and military turmoil. In fact it would be fair to say the World was going politically mad and was in a shambles. The Western countries constantly saw, (imaginary or otherwise), military threats. These threats appeared to come from Russia and her allies in Europe and Asia. So National Service was to extend many years after the war and there was destined to be a British military presence in many overseas lands in which we had interests. Another aspect was that we had a large munitions industry which could not change to the production of non military products overnight. On reflection it must have been politically attractive to successive governments to allow military service to carry on longer than really necessary as it helped to maintain full employment. Apart from perhaps being a little cynical and over simplifying the background of National Service, I believe I have given the brief facts truthfully.

National Service, (after the war), was sexist. By this I mean that in the years after the war until the cessation of compulsory National Service, it only related to men. I don't recall any protests from women's libbers, equal rights campaigners, bra burners or do gooders of a similar ilk shouting that National Service was unfair to females. I submit that there are two possible reasons for this lack of what would now be considered normal demonstration.

1. The groups I have mentioned above, plus the loony left, didn't

exist at the time.

OR

2. They considered it a situation in which it was best to keep a low profile and say 'nowt'. If this was the case, they were certainly blessed with more sense and credibility than they are now.

To keep the record straight, a considerable number of females joined the armed services during this time. Many of them built good careers and carried out important duties next to their male colleagues. I personally have a great admiration for those ladies, particularly as each of them volunteered to serve and advanced in their careers by hard work and personal abilities. All this with no help from the flag waving and often noisy feminine activists of later years. Ruddy good show. It is worthy of mention that in the early days of National Service there was an option to military service. This was achieved by becoming a 'Bevan Boy'. I'll explain. Coal was our main source of energy, at times demand would be considerably higher than output. The fiery labour MP for Ebbw Vale, Aneurin Bevan hit on the idea of drafting men into the mines as an alternative to military service. Hence, 'Bevan Boys'. Having visited an old style mine in the Rhondda during 1992 and gone 300 feet underground, I am thankful that I did my National Service in the RAF. I must add that the experience of going under- ground heightens my admiration for the miners of past and present. The objective of this book is to enlighten, entertain and hopefully amuse. SO PLEASE READ ON

ROYAL AIRFORCE EXPRESSIONS AND SLANG

Some of these expressions would have been (and no doubt still are) common to all branches of the armed services, with the obvious minor amendments to adapt them to a particular branch or situation.

'Get some in', normally said to one with less service than the speaker.

'Get yer knees brown', same as get some in.

'Your number's still wet', same as get some in.

'Sprog', same as get some in.

'FFI', free from infection, medical inspect of private parts.

'Short arm inspection', slang expression for FFI.

'Shooting a line', verbally exaggerating.

'BULL', short for 'bullshit', many meanings, such as – shooting a line – cleaning (bulling) kit, barrack room or military establishment in general; painting and bulling of sundry inane objects. Often used as a reply to those shooting a line or to express disbelief at comments from others. An extremely woody and expressive service word and well used in all branches of armed forces.

'Rock apes', RAF regiment members; regiments main task is defence of airfields and RAF establishments.

'Erk-Erc-AC Plonk', all mean the same, aircraftsman second class (AC2), lowest form of life in the airforce.

'Winco', Wing Commander.

'Groupie', Group Captain.
'Wingless wonder', Admin Officer – non flying type.
'Snowdrop', RAF police.
'Flight', a group of personnel, a Flight Sergeant, a collection of aircraft similar to a squadron.
'Chiefie', Chief Technician or Flight Sergeant.
'1250', RAF personnel identification card.
'Last three', last three digits of official service number.
'Fizzer', a charge-disciplinary action.
'252', number of official form used to initiate a charge.
'295', a leave pass.
'Chitty' – 'Chit', a piece of paper that entitles the holder to do whatever is specified on it.
'Skive', to get out of doing something.
'A skiver', a person with an ability to skive and get away with it.
'Cushy', an easy time or task, sometimes referred to as a 'cushy number'.
'MEAF', Middle East Air Force.
'FEAF', Far East Air Force.
'SEAC', South East Asia command.
'Passenger Role', aircraft fitted with seats for passengers.
'Para Role', aircraft rigged to carry and drop para troops.
'SEAC Role', aircraft rigged for SEAC supply drop.
'Roller Conveyor Role', aircraft rigged for heavy supply drop with parachutes and roller conveyor to speed dispatch.
'Housewife', a small canvas pouch containing – needles, cotton and buttons.
'Button stick', a brass device used when buttons and badges are polished to prevent brasso or similar polish getting on one's uniform.
'bog', toilet.
'CO', Commanding Officer.
'US', unservicable.
'AOG', aircraft on ground.
'George', automatic pilot (the best pilot in the service).
'Dicky', Pilot.
'Second Dicky', Second Pilot.
'AQM', Air Quartermaster, (service equivalent of flight steward).
'Gash', spare, extra, surplus.
'Char', tea.

'Wod', bun or bread roll.
'AOC in C', Air Officer Commanding in Chief.
'VD', venereal disease, an unsocial disease which it was not an offence for an airman to have, but an offence for him not to report having it.
'Clap', same as VD.
'Long lingering leprosy', same as VD.
'Dose of the old dog', same as VD.
'S of RT', School of Recruit Training.
'S of TT', School of Technical Training.
'LAC', Leading Aircraftsman.
'SAC', Senior Aircraftsman.
'WO', Warrant Officer, highest non commissioned rank.
'SWO Man', Station Warrant Officer, responsible for all disciplinary activities associated with running of station.
Responsible directly CO, in some cases is treated on par with God.
'TIN room', the area in which all cooking pans had to be cleaned and stored. The tin room duty was one of the worst fatigues duties that befell an airman.
'Old sweats', long serving, long served or retired service personnel.
'Goolie Chit', a chit that old sweats did a lot of line shooting about. It was 'alleged' that airmen who served in desert areas of the Middle East between the two World Wars carried a goolie chit. This chit was allegedly printed in the Arab dialects of the region and made certain promises of financial reward, on certain conditions. It was a custom of certain Arab tribes at the time to carry out unpleasant alterations to the anatomy of male captives. The chit promise was that any airman who got lost and was returned safely to the British Authorities, his Arab finder would be financially rewarded.
'Form 700', aircraft service record book.
'Square Bashing', basic training.
'Respirator', gas mask.
'Gas Tank', same as respirator.
'IC', in charge.
'Tapes', stripes.
'Gongs', medals.
'Ribbons', medal ribbons.
'Haystack', Handley Page 'Hastings' aircraft.
'Pig', 'Valetta' aircraft.

'AWOL', absent without leave.

'Adrift', same as AWOL.

'23.59 hours', one minute to midnight, (reminds one of Cinderella).

'Scrambled Egg', the gold braid on the peak of an officer's cap.

'UT', under training.

'MT', motor transport.

'MU', maintenance unit.

'Wizard', good – first class.

'Ruddy Good Show', same as wizard.

'A1', same as wizard.

'PTI', Physical training instructor (service equivalent of torturer).

'DI', Drill instructor, personally believed them to have had their brains replaced by the drill manual and numerous instruction books that had deprived them of the ability to think and behave like normal rational humans.

'Shitehawk', the albatross depicted on an airmans shoulder badge.

'Webbing', heavy canvas type of material used for belts, rifle sling, bayonet frog, bags, packs, gaiters and other assorted bits too numerous to mention.

'Blanco', foul sticky paste with the texture of poor quality shoe polish, blue or white for RAF use. Mainly used to 'bull up' webbing.

'Irons', knife, fork and spoon.

'Brylcream Boys', name unfairly given to airmen as a result of recruiting posters depicting an airman with a hair style similar to what was depicted in Brylcream advertisements.

'NAAFI', Navy, Army, Airforce Institute – provided recreational, canteen and shopping facilities.

'SallyAnn', (Red Shield), Salvation Army, provided good basic recreational and canteen facilities with no strings attached.

'AGS Parts', (Aircraft General Standards) This was a guarantee that the parts supplied and used, (even a humble washer) were of the correct specification and standard for which they would be used.

'Gen', Genuine, authentic information as opposed to a line shoot.

'SRO', station routine orders.

'SSO', station or squadron standing orders.

'POR', personnel occurrence report.

'Arrival Chit', a chit or chitty that was issued to an airman when he reported to HQ upon his arrival at a new posting. The chit contained personal details and had to be presented at and signed by all station sections that had reason to know that the airman named in the chit had joined the station's establishment.

'Departure Chit', Arrival chit in reverse.

'Prop', propeller.

'Avgas', aviation gasoline, (high octane petrol).

'Avtur', aviation turbine fuel.

'Avtag', aviation turbine gasoline.

'Kerosene', paraffin.

'C of E', Church of England.

'O.D.', Other denominations, (not C of E, Catholics or Jews).

'TSF', transport support flight.

'TDF', transport development flight.

'TSE', transport support element.

'POM', dehydrated potato, runny, pale and totally tasteless. Bears no resemblance to the brands now available.

'Aerodrome', Military airfield.

'Drome', Same as aerodrome.

'Dispersal', External parking area for aircraft. AT SOME DISTANCE

'Apron', ~~same as dispersal~~. AREA IN FRONT OF HANGER

'Taxiway', roads over which aircraft move between dispersal and runway.

'PSP', pressed steel plate, large sections (about 2' x 6') of perforated steel plate. Resembled oversized Meccano sections which could be quickly linked together to form temporary roads or hard standing. Even used for airstrips.

Chapter 1

THE FIRST STEP

When I left technical school at the age of sixteen years, it was to start work with Morris Commercial Cars as an apprentice in their Adderley Park (Birmingham) factory, at 25/= per week (£1.25). Like all lads of my age I realised that I would have a commitment to military service at some future date. I can say in all honesty that I settled into my work routine with enthusiasm and was happier than I have ever been at school. The thought of National Service occupied a very minor place in the back of my mind and I gave it little thought. I was progressing in my training, earning a little more; most importantly I met a young lady by the name of Mary and started courting her. I was jolted back to reality shortly before my eighteenth birthday when I realised it was almost time for me to register for National Service. On the appointed Saturday morning, I presented myself at Small Heath Labour Exchange to sign on the dotted line for Queen and Country. After ~~signing up~~ and indicating that I would like to serve in the RAF, I formally applied for deferment of service. This was to allow me to complete my apprenticeship and studies as a day release student for a City and Guilds qualification in motor engineering. Shortly after signing up I heard that my deferment was approved. With this knowledge I was again able to push thoughts of National Service to the back of my mind and get on with living life in a civilised manner. I gained more experience in my trade training and college studies. Mary and I became engaged and in 1954 we married, I was twenty years old, Mary was nineteen.

In February 1955 I attained the age of twenty one, completed my

we were not required to sign

apprenticeship and became a skilled fitter/mechanic in the experimental department at Morris Commercial Cars. As near as I can recall the rate of pay at that time for a skilled improver was in the region of £10 for a forty hour week, with a 7.30 a.m. start. Another important event occurred in February 1955, Mary and I bought our first house. A very pleasant three bedroomed semi in Olton for the princely sum of £1700, at 4% interest, with mortgage repayments of £8-0-6 (£8.02 p) per month; 'Oh how times change'.

Shortly after this reality took a hand and I was summoned to attend my medical and selection interview for National Service. If any of you have ever heard the entertainer Jasper Carrott do his skit on a BBC medical, the one I had was even more bizarre than he relates. I passed my medical grade one, I was then able to carry on with a normal life until at some date I would receive my summons to report. Shortly before I had my medical the period of service was increased from eighteen months to two years, so I was going to have to do an extra period of service.

I carried on with life as normally as possible whilst I waited apprehensively for my summons to serve Queen and Country. 4th July is etched in my mind for ever and for several unrelated reasons. It is American Independence Day, I got engaged on July 4th 1951, it is also the birthday of my dear wife. July 4th 1955 was Mary's twenty first birthday. Amongst the post that arrived on that special day was a large brown envelope addressed to me and bearing the letters OHMS on the envelope. You have no doubt guessed, it contained my calling up papers. What a day for that document, that was destined to disrupt our lives for two years, to arrive. It was in fact a classical example of what is commonly known as 'sods law'. The envelope contained instructions for me to report to RAF Cardington, Bedfordshire on July 19th 1955, it also contained a travel warrant which would allow me to travel by British Railways from Birmingham to Bedford, third class, of course.

Chapter 2

PREPARATION

I had finally been shocked out of complacency about National Service and would have to pull my finger out during what would prove to be a hectic couple of weeks. I was not to be alone in reporting to Cardington as my friend, Brian Heard had received the same call up date as me. Brian and I had attended technical school together for two years, left on the same day to become apprentices with the same company. We were in fact destined to remain friends until Brian's premature death in 1991. But back to the preparation of that time. I had to give notice at work. My job was protected by law for my eventual return to civilian life. Things would be difficult for Mary as we had a house of our own and, of course, the mortgage that went with it. Fortunately Mary was and still is not frightened of hard work, in fact she is blessed with a determination to succeed that becomes stronger with obstacles that would be disastrous to lesser beings. I recall that we made application for National Service grant. This was a small welfare payment that was supposed to assist National Service men to meet financial obligations that had not proved a problem when they received civilian wages. We believed that we may well have been entitled to some assistance with our mortgage payments whilst I was in the RAF. How wrong could we be? The interviewer listened to us and then pronounced that as we had no children, hire purchase debts and Mary was a healthy young woman who could go to work, our entitlement would be nil. Obviously some things never change, as it seems that those who pay the most into the kitty have the most difficult job of getting some out of it when it's most needed.

Having said my farewells to colleagues and friends, with sadness as it was to be an absence of two years, with my luck I would not have been surprised if the Politicians and Whitehall Warriors had chosen to increase the period of service. Fortunately they didn't. I visited the local hairdresser the day before I reported and had a very short respectable haircut in the hope that it would avoid me having to have a recruits trim when I reported. What I had seen of military haircuts made them more suitable to serving prisoners than people who had sworn an oath of allegiance to the Queen.

324, Lyndon Road. The home I left to report for National Service.

Chapter 3

THE START

July 19th 1955, the day that was to be the start of a new experience for me. The day I was destined to cease to be a civilian. The day I was to become an AC plonk. Me who had survived the trials and tribulations of five years as an apprentice was about to start all over again on the bottom rung. Well and truly at the tail end of the pecking order. It was also the day that would see my wife, at a mere twenty one years of age, assume responsibility of head of the house. Not for her the support, counselling and other assorted crap that now appears to be the norm for servicemen's wives. She was left to her own devices to manage as best she could.

The home atmosphere on that morning almost forty years ago was, to the best of my memory, very subdued and quiet. Mary and I set out together from our home and walked the half mile to get a bus to the City (Birmingham). We waited for the bus near the Sheldon cinema, a place in which we had spent many happy hours and would again when I returned from National Service. As instructed I travelled light, with just my personal necessities in a grip bag. This bag would eventually be used to pack all my civilian clothes in for sending home when I was kitted out with my uniform. The bus took us along Coventry Road, through Small Heath on our journey to the city. It is worth relating how different the Coventry Road was at that time to how it is now. There seemed to be hundreds of small family shops (all thriving), the road was fairly narrow by today's standards and still had a cobbled stone surface at Hay Mills. The main land mark at Small Heath was the massive Singer car factory, which withstood the bombing of the Second World War, but like so much of our social and industrial heritage eventually fell prey to the planners and disappeared to make way for a monstrosity of a supermarket. The other point that shows how drastic the changes have been is that from the bus in 1955 we passed no fewer than six thriving cinemas between Sheldon and Bordesley. There are now none. Our bus arrived at the Bull Ring and we alighted in Moor Street. A short walk across the Bull Ring, which at that time had a lethal cobbled surface as it had done for the preceding few hundred years and with its abundance of market traders and barrow boys was still the traditional heart of Birmingham. No time to linger on that fateful day, I had a tight schedule to answer the call of Queen and Country. Personally I would have preferred not to have had the call in the first place. After crossing the Bull Ring we went along Bell Street, between the fish market and the shell of the old market hall. This brought us to Queens Drive, a long straight cobble stoned road that ran through the centre of New Street station, to Navigation Street. New Street station, was in 1955, a large old smoke grimed building of great character that was well worn by time and neglect of the war years. Nevertheless it was a much loved building that had over the years witnessed many sad partings and happy reunions. We met up with Brian, he was accompanied by Vera, who was to shortly become his wife. I think both Brian and I were pleased that Vera and Mary would have the support of each other when we departed. Our train arrived and we boarded it with several other new recruits, some of whom Brian and I knew well as we had attended the City and Guilds course with them at Aston Technical College.

As the train departed, everyone who had a loved one to see them off wanted to be by an open window to hold a hand to the last possible moment. Being a fairly big guy I managed to get one of the limited window places and recall Mary and I waving until the train took us out of sight of each other. The atmosphere in the carriage was subdued and deathly quiet as each of us settled down with our own personal thoughts during the journey to Bedford. As I recall the journey was made without having to change trains. This can't be done now as a result of the decimation of our rail system by Dr Beeching. As I stated earlier the group in the compartment became totally absorbed with their individual thoughts. Some of the men who had young families no doubt worried as to how wives and children would cope in their absence. Some must have had grave misgivings about what was going to happen to them, particularly if they had never spent any time away from home. My own thoughts centred on my wife and what was the first enforced absence since we had married over a year before. I had no doubts that I was well equipped to handle any situations that I would have to face during the next couple of years, with the experience of over six years of factory work, plus two years voluntary work as a special constable. Added to this as a lad I'd been away from home on numerous camping and youth hostelling jaunts. I was worldly enough to survive and no doubt prosper, given the chances. I had no doubts about how Mary would manage; in her short life she had suffered some knocks but had risen above adversity and come out on top. It did seem unfair though that we could not prosper together. When I had all these thoughts during that fateful journey I silently hoped that I would get a home posting so that we could at least spend a small amount of time together. On reflection the philosophy we adopted at that time was right, and its continued use over the years has served us well during those times and difficult situations.

When the train arrived at Bedford there seemed to be hundreds of young men alighting from it, all enroute to RAF Cardington. There was no time for thought or bewilderment as the new recruits seemed to be outnumbered by Admin Orderlies, who looked so bored that they did little to enhance the image of the RAF. At that moment I came to the conclusion that Corporal Admin Orderlies had bigger mouths than they had brains. I can say with all sincerity that nothing occurred during the following two years to make me change my opinion.

Eventually a Sergeant with a commanding personality and voice to match, arrived on the scene. From that moment things began to fall into place with a near to military precision, or as near to military precision as was possible with a bunch of raw and reluctant recruits. With the exception of the odd demented person amongst us, I am sure that each one of us could have thought of more desirable places than listening to some moron shouting out orders on Bedford railway station. But it was something we all learned to accept during the next few weeks at our various training establishments. The Bedford station experience was to be a very gentle experience of what was to come.

We were eventually ushered out of the station towards service coaches. Bedford utilities, obviously. This was for the final stage of our journey to RAF Cardington. As I stepped onto the coach, Brian was immediately behind me. A hand went out behind me to indicate that I was to be the last person to board, as the coach was full. From that moment on the careers of Brian and I followed different paths. We went to different square bashing camps, trained in different trades and ultimately got postings that separated us even more for the duration of our service.

Brian went to Akrotiri in Cyprus as an armourer, whilst I became an aero engine mechanic in a squadron that had its home base at Abingdon on Thames, which at that time was in Berkshire and not Oxfordshire as it is now.

Author (4th from left, front row), with other 'Raw' recruits. RAF Cardington, July 1955

Chapter 4

RAF CARDINGTON

The first sight of RAF Cardington was very impressive. This was due to the station's most famous feature dominating the Bedfordshire countryside, as it had done for many years. What was this feature that so impressed? It was the airship hangar. A grand relic of the period in which we competed with Germany to build and operate the largest and grandest airships, a period in which both countries believed the future of civil and military aviation lay in airships. The Second World War and history proved this theory wrong; but back to reality and that eventful day in July 1955.

There was little else special about RAF Cardington. It was typical of many other large service establishments. It had the usual large warehouse style hangars, endless rows of very dated wooden huts with highly polished (bulled up) lino covered floors. Many acres of well manicured grassed areas and of course literally hundreds of white painted useless inate objects, yes, Cardington was a good example of a military establishment. Some service personnel may say that things are still the same now, who knows? I for one am fortunately not in a position to comment.

I was to be at Cardington for about one week, this was the normal time for kitting out and processing. I found out that the day a new recruit started processing was of some importance. The reason being that it took a specific number of days to pass through the system and recruits left for different schools of recruit training, (square bashing camps) on specific days of the week. So it was possible to make a guesstimate of one's basic training camp. I calculated that mine could well be Bridgnorth. My calculation was infact correct, but more of that later. Cardington proved to be an extremely gentle introduction to service life. The routine was casual, possibly made more so by the attitude of many of the Admin Orderlies who where not the brightest of persons. During my brief stay at this camp there was to be an inspection by the AOC in C. As new recruits our specific instruction for his visit was to 'bull up' our billets and keep out of his way. Needless to say we heeded this order, particularly the latter part. I remember particularly that this AOC had a hyphenated name which seemed one hundred percent plus in keeping with his service position. The name just rolled off the tongue and with one extra word added was even more appropriate. This name that is forever etched in my memory was 'Fuller Bull'. Need I say more? The first task for recruits was a visit to the camp barber. I think a better term for the persons actually carrying out the haircutting would be butchers. We lined up outside the barber's hut, it was a large hut which had an entrance at the top of a flight of four or five steps. As we lined up at the foot of these steps the man in charge of the establishment stood in the doorway of the hut, hands on hips and with a look of utter contempt on his face he looked us over. My immediate reaction was to mumble to myself 'ruddy civilian', I was already beginning the process of changing into a serviceman. But back to the butcher, sorry barber. His eyes lit up when he spotted a recruit with long blond hair. With the words of 'come with me primrose', he led him into the hut and handed him over to the apprentice barber like the proverbial sacrificial lamb. The apprentice did his best, which by civilised standards was pathetic, by the time the head butcher completed a salvage job on what little hair the hapless recruit had left he was nigh on bald. I must confess to uttering a silent prayer as my respectable short haircut had spared me an unpleasant ordeal at the hands of some demented demon barber.

The hut I was billeted in was one in a long row and looked onto a large open grassed area, on this area was one solitary isolated hut. It was obviously put there to keep its inmates isolated from the rest of humanity. If you think I'm going to say the inmates were isolated because of some terrible contagious disease, you couldn't be more wrong. It was infact the band room. Most RAF stations had a volunteer band. The ability of these bands in my humble non musically educated opinion varied considerably, however, I must concede that the RAF Cardington band was the worst I ever heard. To be in my billet when the band practised was akin to torture no doubt contrived by some wingless wonder at the Air Ministry who saw it as an additional way of subjecting new recruits to a little extra discomfort.

As the days progressed we continued our transformation from civilians to airmen. Uniforms and allied equipment was issued and duly stamped, stencilled or marked in some way with our newly acquired service number, which for the next two years was to be more important than our names. I am quite sure that, given the opportunity the orderlies who wielded the number stamps and foul smelling ink pads would have numbered our bodies as well as our kit. When the issue of uniforms had been completed we had the unpleasant task of packing all our civilian clothes and posting them home. That I think was when it hit each and every one of us that we had now ceased to be civilians. We had to attend several medical examinations and lectures. One of the topics that was laboured at these lectures was to sing the praises of signing on for a longer term of service, with an added incentive of the higher pay rate. A few naive souls fell for the speil, most muttered obscenities such as 'go forth and multiply' or words to that effect. We were informed that when the time came for us to move to our respective training camps, it would be necessary to travel in full marching order. So next came full instructions and demonstrations of how to present ourselves in this somewhat antiquated method of service dress. Firstly to assemble the various items of webbing it was necessary to refer back to instructions that would have been more appropriate to an infantry man who was preparing to go to the front during World War One; so much for progress. The total assembly of the webbing consisted of putting together the following pieces of equipment. Belt, two shoulder straps, two ammunition pouches, large back pack, small side pack and a water bottle. The crowning glory was to balance a kit bag on the top of the back pack like a ruddy great stencilled carbuncle. It was compulsory when attired in this lot to wear a peaked cap, which the kit bag tried to dislodge. When our kit was issued it had been made clear to us that the flat cap should not be modified in any way, either by altering the peak as Guardsmen did, or by bending the top and front to resemble a Gestapo officer's hat.

Although I did note during my service career many snowdrops altered their hats in the latter way, no doubt the poor demented little persons thought this modification gave them an appearance of authority. Infact the effect was the opposite, it made them look even more pathetic, if that was possible.

There was a brief visit to the station tailor's shop to ensure the reasonable fit of uniforms before the general public was permitted to set their eyes on us. My time at Cardington drew towards its close and I was informed that I would be posted to number Seven School of Recruit Training at RAF Bridgnorth to complete my transformation from civilian to airman. Brian was not so fortunate with his posting as he was to go onto RAF Padgate near Warrington. So it was forward to the next phase, not without a certain amount of trepidation on my part.

Guard Room – RAF Bridgnorth. Recruits had to pass scrutiny here before being allowed out of camp.

Chapter 5

IN TRANSIT

(FIRST TIME)

I awoke on that eventful day in the distant past. The day that was to be the start of the second stage of my transformation from a happy civilian to a reluctant AC Plonk in the service of her Majesty. It was a beautiful summer morning, the type of morning holiday makers dream about. It was a pity that on such a morning as this, there would be a large number of morons about who seemed to have the express task of preventing recruits having time to enjoy what mother nature had to offer; that's life. Although none of us knew what to expect, there was a certain excitement in the air. We had spent our last night at RAF Cardington and would soon be taking the next step that would hopefully take us one stage closer to the real operational airforce. After breakfast it was necessary to spend time on essential military duties such as handing in bedding and bulling the billet in preparation for the next bunch of poor souls who would use it. At last we paraded in full marching order, hopefully to be complemented on our smart military bearing. I must admit we were totally unprepared for what was to come. Oh what a shock when we lined up on parade. We had got used to the Cardington parades being taken by a collection of scruffy Admin Orderlies. This parade was different, very different. It was taken by four Corporals who resembled Guardsmen in their immaculately tailored uniforms and peaked caps. It soon became obvious that they had the commanding voices to match their appearance. After looking us over their faces betrayed their feelings, that they thought us to resemble something rather unpleasant that had been brought in by a shortsighted cat. They didn't hurry; this scrutiny infact took two or three minutes, standing there it felt a lot longer. The spokesman for the quartet then drew himself up to his full height, pushed out his chest, looked over us once more with a contemptuous frown and then spoke his piece. He informed us we looked an offensive shower, or words to that effect. He went on to say that he and his colleagues had come from RAF Bridgnorth to escort us to that establishment and there attempt to turn us into presentable and useful members of the RAF. He was, as were his three companions Drill Instructors. He went on to say that having seen us for the first time, their immediate thought was to desert and enlist in the French Foreign Legion. They however decided against that action as it would be an admission of defeat. I must admit that this nameless Corporal had a sense of the dramatic and the gift of uttering the most credible of verbal abuse. I came to the immediate conclusion that regardless of how well, or poorly, he rated as a DI he was worthy of ten out of ten for bull shooting. He went on to say that as our appearance may well offend the eyes of the more sensitive members of the civilian population, (at least the implication was that we we airmen), we would not travel to Bedford to board our train for Bridgnorth. We would march to a remote railway halt that was a short distance away over the fields at the rear of RAF Cardington. Somewhat dejected after the first of our verbal onslaughts we set off on the short march to the railway. Shortly after our arrival at the station the train appeared. It is hardly fair to refer to it as a train, an apparition is perhaps a better description, it was of course what British Railways presented at that time. A locomotive that had been the pride of some driver in the distant past but was alas now handicapped by what appeared to be several tons of soot and miscellaneous filth encrusted on it. This was not the worst; the locomotive was pulling about a dozen old style LMS coaches. These coaches had been painted, (very poorly) at some time in BR livery and worst of all, every single coach was of the non corridor type. Yes, the train was typical of what was on offer to the travelling public, and still is. Some things never change. The train was boarded with a degree of relief as it was now possible to put our kit bags down and remove our webbing equipment, which we had worn for about two hours. I only recall brief details of that long past journey. It was by a roundabout route as it lasted from about 10.30 a.m. until 4.00 p.m. The train made one brief stop at some remote country station, obviously by prior arrangement, as trolleys had been lined up on the platform loaded with food and tea. The food was welcome, in spite of it being such a hot bright day, most declined the tea due to the lack of toilet facilities on the train. The journey was via Northampton, Coventry, Birmingham, Dudley, Bewdley and up the picturesque Severn Valley line to Bridgnorth. I had done the trip from Birmingham to Bewdley on many earlier and happier occasions with my wife.

The train arrived at Bridgnorth and we all disboarded, in full kit of course. The order was then given to form up in three lines in the railway station forecourt, still in full kit in spite of the mid afternoon heat. The concession was made that kit bags could be lowered and stood on the floor, this of course provided bags stood upright in the attention position. At this point I noticed we were being scrutinised from all sides by large numbers of people who had nothing better to do than watch us whilst they enjoyed the pleasant summer day out. No doubt they found our style of dress and behaviour bizarre in the extreme. Ruddy civilians

Other watchers posed more of a threat than did the civilian tourists. There other watchers appeared as we formed up in to ranks. Each one of them wore RAF battle dress uniforms that appeared to have been exclusively tailored for them. They also wore service peaked caps which had been modified so that the peaks almost touched the tip of the wearers nose. Infact each and every one of them looked mean. These persons were more of the DI's who for the next few weeks would dominate most of our time. In fairness the behaviour of most of them, (note most) was a facade and they mellowed considerably as we neared the end of our training. There were infact to be five or six tough weeks to survive before this stage was reached. It was at this point I experienced my first example of discrimination in service life. RAF coaches had by now arrived on the scene, obviously to convey recruits to RAF Bridgnorth. A 'portly' Flight Sergeant bawled out the order, 'regular airmen fall out, national servicemen stand fast'. The regulars boarded the coaches whilst the rest of us obediently did as ordered. Not a solitary voice sounded in dissent, no doubt about it, we'd learned a lot in a week.

The coaches eventually returned, together with several canvas covered service wagons. These vehicles then conveyed the remainder of us to our new temporary home at RAF Bridgnorth, Shropshire.

RAF Bridgnorth Station Badge.

Chapter 6

RAF BRIDGNORTH

(ARRIVAL AND FIRST IMPRESSIONS)

My arrival at the gates of number seven School of Recruit Training was unceremonious. It was in the back of a Bedford military truck. I was packed into this vehicle so tightly that it was impossible to raise an arm to hold onto any part of the roof frame for support. This however was of little consequence as being packed so tightly in the vertical position made it unnecessary to hold on. This of course was an advantage as it did prevent us from falling over, in spite of the worst efforts of the vehicle's driver. The journey was fortunately only of a short duration, just as well, as after the number of hours we had spent travelling in the heat every one of us was hot, sweaty, thoroughly brassed off and desperately in need of a pee. Not the most pleasant set of conditions for travelling companions. It was obvious that my first view, (as an Airman) of number 7 S of RT would be very limited as it was going to be through the rear of the canvas tilt on a Bedford wagon. To keep the record correct, I had briefly visited this RAF station on an earlier occasion. That was 1948, when I called there whilst on a cycling trip. The purpose of that visit was to call on an old friend of the family who was a Flight Sergeant in the Rock Apes and on detachment as a Combat Instructor. But back to my unceremonious arrival as a raw recruit. The vehicle I was in swept through the gates, which of course with my blinkered view of the back of the vehicle I didn't see until we were well past them and within the confines of the tall, barbed wire topped mesh fence. I was later to find out that this particular fence was a charade as like so many other military establishments the rear of the premises was protected by a very threadbare and sparse hedge, in many places less than three feet tall. The vehicle eventually pulled up. Not before the demon driver had subjected us to the discomfort of swaying round a few more corners. The backboard was dropped with a resounding bump and a Corporal whom I had not seen before, shouted 'get out'. We were destined to see a lot of this Corporal during the next few weeks. I remember him well. He was a long service man with a particular bitter and twisted outlook. I can perhaps sum him up as an ignorant, moronic person. He was only possibly promoted on the sympathetic whim of some wingless wonder desk pilot who misguidedly thought his loyal service warranted a pair of stripes.

We jumped out of the vehicle only to be immediately bawled at by our newly found moronic Corporal, 'get back in that ruddy motor.' Why? Because the driver of the vehicle had erred and parked in a position that caused his reluctant passengers to alight onto sacred ground. Infact as we jumped out our feet had contaminated the edge of the parade square; a piece of gravel covered earth that we would soon discover was there for the express purpose of inflicting the maximum degree of discomfort on recruits. So this was to be my home for the next few weeks. A piece of hallowed ground and a bed in a wooden oversize garden shed.

Roll on demob.

Chapter 7

RAF BRIDGNORTH

(THE FIRST FEW HOURS)

I'd arrived, looked, digested and as there was no option, decided to settle in and make the best of it. At least this particular training establishment was within about one hour's travelling time of home and not in some remote location at the other end of the country. The remainder of that first day was to be hectic as it would be used in getting organised for what was to commence the following day. The first task was to get into a billet, complete with kit. The first rule when entering a billet was to treat the highly polished floor as sacred and not walk on it. Those readers who have had the experience of a square bashing (basic training) establishment will appreciate the effort that was put into attaining the glass like finish on billet floors. The occupants of a billet would go to considerable trouble and personal inconvenience to maintain the surface in an attempt to make floor bulling a little easier. You will appreciate that the coming and going of about forty airmen in service issue hob nailed boots would play havoc with a highly polished floor. So the rule was, don't walk on the floor. Before you conjure up a mental picture of a crowd of airmen walking on their hands I will explain. Inside the door of the billet was a little pile of square dusters cut from old blankets. By stepping onto a couple of these squares, it was not only possible to slide about the billet, the floor got an additional polish. The more lethal the floor surface the happier it made the bull happy administration, funny people. Things don't change much do they? We still seem to have a high percentage of funny folk in responsible positions.

When the hut I had been allocated was full, the DI in charge made himself known to us. He also made it known that there would be no escape from him as he had a small private room, (a bunk) within the billet. He then marched us to collect bedding, demonstrated the service way of making up a bed pack for daily display and of course the method that we would have to adopt to make a bed up to sleep in. This ritual was to be adhered to on a daily basis, what a load of bull. It was then made known to us that as it was getting close to the August Bank Holiday, (this holiday used to always be the first weekend in August), and it was normal in the RAF to given airmen a few days leave, (the August grant). It was made clear that as recruits we would not get the grant as a right; however we might get it subject to certain conditions. The DI then took a great delight in putting the pressure on by outlining these terms in minute detail.

1. It would be necessary to excel in all aspects of training during our first week.
2. We must wear our uniforms in a way that would not make us offensive to the civilian population.
3. We must know who to salute and be able to do it in a correct manner.
4. We must not attract the attention of military or civilian police.

If we managed to meet those conditions plus several other items of trivia we may get some leave, big deal. So the carrot had been well and truly dangled, the pressure was on, no doubt many reminders would be issued during the next few days. At this stage it was time to eat, thank goodness, my belly was beginning to think that my throat had been cut. Getting to the airmen's mess was to be a monumental military operation. We would have to march, infact it was normal for recruits to be marched to and from the mess during the first two weeks of training. The ritual was to form up in three ranks on the apron outside the billet. When formed up to the satisfaction of the DI we would then be marched to the mess, irons had to be clasped in the left hand, which was bent round so that the irons were tucked neatly into the carrier's back. All this was very military, infact it was a good example of over the top bull. When going through this particular ritual for the first time I did wonder if the gastronomical delights that would be offered would be worth the trouble; wouldn't you? I have never quite grasped how this infantile type of ritual would assist in making raw recruits into useful members of the RAF. Fortunately for myself and my contemporaries of the time we had already accepted the wisdom of the old saying 'ours is not to reason why – ours is but to do and die', this was to prove a sound philosophy during square bashing. After my first meal at Bridgnorth I had to admit that I had been very pleasantly surprised how good it was. In fairness I must admit that I rarely had cause to criticise the food that was served to me during my time in the RAF. Service food had been at the butt of comedians' jokes for many years, no doubt some service personnel had suffered from horrific food at times, possibly due to the efforts of ill trained and unqualified cooks. When I went into the RAF catering was a recognised career and taken very seriously by the long service personnel employed in that branch. There was also a large number of National Service men who had served apprenticeships in catering prior to being called up. The two groups integrated well and pursued their skills for the benefit of all who used RAF messes. The only real point I can make in criticism is that I never got used to having runny dehydrated potato, (POM) on offer at all meals, including breakfast. Ugh.

After that first meal at Bridgnorth it was back to the billet, (marched of course) and an evening sorting kit and finding out what would be going on during the next few weeks of 'square bashing'. The Corporal IC the billet, who was fortunately to prove himself to be intellectually superior to many of his moronic comrades, was to spend the entire evening with us. It was to be a busy, but useful evening which would hopefully get us off on the right foot for what was to come. The things dealt with on that summer evening of nearly forty years ago were varied in the extreme. I'll try to list them, but of course my memory is a little vague on some aspects.

Basic training was normally for eight weeks, however, as the August Bank Holiday would intervene my particular flight would have to do nine weeks. For the first part of training, as a junior flight normal dress would be, collar and tie, (stiff well starched detachable collar) working blues with well pressed trousers, shirt sleeve order before six p.m., beret with well polished badge and tightly adjusted webbing belt, duly cleaned with blanco and with well polished brass fittings.

Posted on the billet wall was a copy of the training timetable. It showed clearly that our days would be full and evenings would be mostly occupied in the serious military duty of bulling up personal kit and billets. The training would consist of basic traditional drill, (square bashing) firearms drill, physical training, combat training, education and lectures on service related and matters of general interest; the latter loose description was obviously used to cover miscellaneous verbal rubbish. Time was also devoted on that first evening to receiving considerable instruction on how to lay out personal kit on a daily basis for inspection. There was instruction on another major military matter, this was on how to pack webbing bags with cardboard, paper and other sundry tat. What was the object of filling webbing bags in this way? It was obviously to make them take up more space and gather more dust when not in use. That's my theory and I'm sticking to it, it's better than the reasons given for some of the ruddy silly things I had to do during square bashing.

The day finally came to an end with the instruction to parade for breakfast at 7.30 a.m. the following morning. This was of course after having a wash and shave, bulling the billet and generally dashing round in ever decreasing circles.

The die was cast, the pattern was set, roll on demob.

Chapter 8

ASPECTS OF SQUARE BASHING – FIRST STAGE

I have no desire to have my recollections of square bashing read like a diary or documentary. With this in mind I have decided to write briefly on a potpourri of experiences as I recall them. This way excuses me the need to list events in their precise sequence. The first two weeks of training was very intense and the members of my flight stood out as the newest of new boys. When we marched, (as we did to everywhere except the bog and NAAFI) we had to swing our arms to shoulder height. In addition to this we suffered the added indignity of having to shout out the timing of each and every drill movement we were ordered to carry out. One dress concession we were allowed at Bridgnorth was that recruits did not have to wear gaiters. DI's and Snowdrops always wore gaiters when on duty. It is worth mentioning that when these persons wore gaitors, their trousers always hung perfectly evenly over their gaiters. I found out that this was achieved by weighing down the bottom of their trouser legs with rings of motor cycle chain; a classic example of bull.

During this early period we learned to change from one form of dress to another in double quick time, lost some weight, got physically fit, ate well and slept well. The latter as a result of being totally knackered at the end of the day. In fact we all changed rapidly during those two weeks. During this period we acquired one major additional piece of equipment to cherish and keep clean. Namely an Enfield 303 rifle, purely for drill purposes. These rifles were so ancient that if anybody had been foolish enough to use live ammunition in them there is little doubt that they would have blown up. When we drew these ancient firearms from the armoury we had no idea of how to shoulder or slope arms. The DI's made it clear that it was forbidden to carry rifles as one would carry a shotgun if one was a farmer out to bag a few rabbits, (the terminology used was a little more flowery than I have used). The order was to short trail them. Anybody who has had to carry an Enfield rifle for any distance at the short trail will vouch for how wearing it is. The method consisted of keeping the arm straight down the side with the first finger hooked into the trigger guard, thus the full weight of the rifle was taken by one finger hooked into the trigger guard. There was also a visit to the tailor's shop for basic alterations to our best uniforms in preparation for when we would eventually be allowed off camp. Considerable time had to be spent each evening getting the desired glass like finish on the toe caps of our boots. No mean task as service issue boots started life with a bubble finish surface. The most frustrating aspect about boots was that the toe caps got badly scored during each day of training, but the high standard of finish was demanded each morning on parade. During these first days of training there were brief respites from the more arduous tasks for the purpose of attending lectures. The content of these lectures was varied, as was the credibility of the people who gave them. Subjects such as writing a letter of grievance to the CO (as if any recruit would dare), the financial advantages of signing on, the accounts wallah (or wally) who gave this talk was far more enthusiastic than his audience. Two of the lectures however are firmly etched in my memory and I believe are worthy of being put into print for posterity. The first was a lecture on the rights and privileges of the recruit which was scheduled to be of thirty minutes duration. We duly assembled in the lecture room and waited; and waited, we waited a total of twenty five minutes. At this point a wingless wonder pilot officer entered. He walked to the front of the room, turned, put his hat and stick on the table, gave those gathered a disdainful look and in a high pitched immature voice said his piece. This consisted of, 'it is my duty to tell you your rights and privileges, as recruits you have f*** all rights and no privileges'. We at least had a rest for half an hour. The other lecture that I wish to specifically mention is the film on VD which was fortunately not in colour. I remember particularly the talk that followed as the MO who gave it had a particularly good spiel. After graphically describing ways in which this particular unsocial disease could be caught, he went on to say that it was not an offence to have the disease, but it was a serious offence not to report having it. He them came to his punch line which was to say, 'it was no good an individual saying he caught it from the toilet seat, as that reason was only accepted from the CO, Padre or MO.'

I still admire that lecturer's use of the English language. The entire flight was confined to camp during that first weekend at Bridgnorth, this was normal as it was compulsory for the junior flight to attend church parade. I imagine a considerable number of civilian clergymen would like captive congregations to fill their churches on Sundays. Part way through the second week of training it was announced that we had attained the necessary minimum standard to be granted home leave for the August bank holiday. In uniform, of course, as civilian clothes had been sent home from Cardington. With the promise of a brief home leave the next few days seemed like an eternity. The weekend arrived and it was home for a few days. The journey from camp to Birmingham was on a coach that had been hired from Whittles and the hit tune of the time, which was 'Unchained Melody' sung by Jimmy Young, was playing on the coach radio. I was luckier than some of my fellow airmen who had homes further from Bridgnorth and would have to spend a considerable amount of their brief leave in travelling. When I alighted from my bus at Sheldon after the short ride from Birmingham City centre, it was a somewhat self conscious airman who walked up his road in uniform. A journey I had made in reverse as a civilian some three weeks earlier. It seemed much longer.

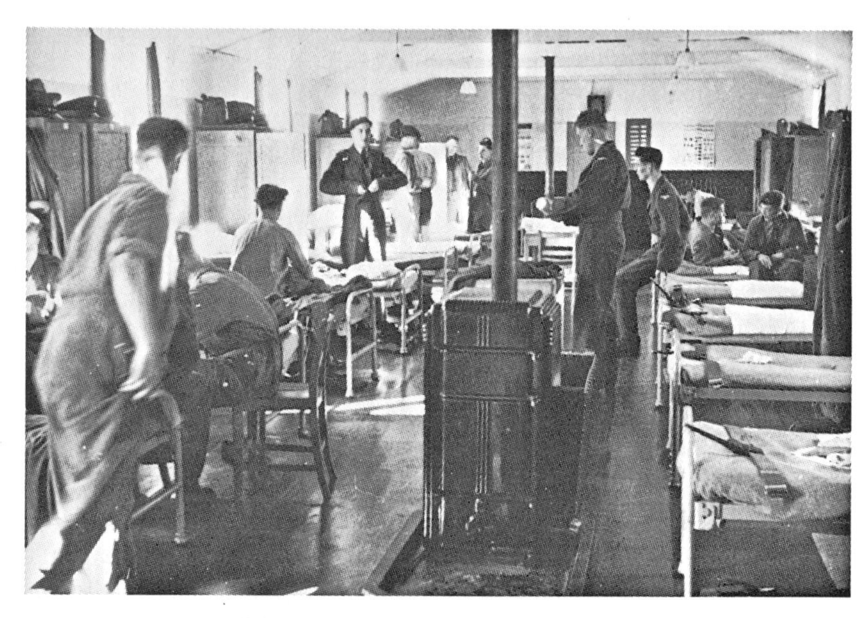

Interior of a typical Bridgnorth billet.
Note the row of Lea Enfield 303 rifles on the far wall, right hand side.

Chapter 9

ASPECTS OF SQUARE BASHING - MIDDLE STAGE - WEEKS THREE, FOUR, FIVE AND SIX.

I returned to RAF Bridgnorth somewhat dejected and generally brassed off after having had the pleasure of a few days of leave and domestic normality. I was able to get some consolation from the fact that I only had in the region of twenty three months of service to complete before discharge; roll on demob. A lot was to be done during the middle four weeks of square bashing. The pace of training was to get more intense, as by the end of this stage my contemporaries and I would be in line to assume the position of senior flight. An awesome position which would require a lot of dedicated preparation. Given a different set of circumstances a lot of pleasure could have been gained from exploring the Worcestershire/Shropshire countryside around the camp. There was certainly no time for pleasures of this kind in 1955; I have however made up for this, not only have I explored the area in connection with my genealogical research. My wife and I have camped in the area many times and come to love the countryside.

We have come to love it so much, that we have our retirement home in Shropshire. At least mother nature was kind to me back in 1955, as to the best of my recollection there was not one wet day during my period of square bashing. This was fortunate as most of the training was outside. I will now deal with some of the things that went on during that critical four weeks in the life of an RAF recruit. The particular phase started with the usual threat of being deflighted if anybody failed to come up to the necessary standard of proficiency. The theory of deflighting was that the offending airman would move back to the following intake of recruits, which would have the result of having to do a specific two weeks of square bashing for a second time. Ugh. I do recall one man being deflighted, in fact it happened to him twice; of course he was a thick beggar and deserved what he got. There was one other young man who disappeared from the scene after a few days of training. His behaviour during those first few days saw him stuck with the nickname of Ethel. On reflection his behaviour would have maybe been more suitable to the female branch of the service. That maybe where he disappeared to; who knows? It is becoming obvious that this chapter is turning into a mini epic; so without any more line shooting, artist's licence etc., I'll get on with it.

Rifle Drill etc.

It was only when this aspect of training commenced that one was able to appreciate the complexities of handling a 303 rifle without even firing it. Thank goodness I did all my rifle drill in the summer and was thus spared the problem of having to handle the damn thing whilst wearing woollen gloves, which obviously didn't help. I later learned that at the time of the year when recruits wore gloves, it was the custom to soak the gloves to improve their gripping qualities. Ugh.

Firstly we mastered handling the rifle whilst standing still. After this we marched with it, (both quick and slow) reversed it and presented it. Drill is basically a group of people carrying out operations collectively in unison with a bit of swank thrown in. One of the tricks we learned was it made the present arms impressive if the magazine on the rifle was left unclipped prior to doing the actual present. As the present was completed the left hand clicked the magazine home at the same moment that the well studded left boot was slammed to the ground. We also learned how to fix and unfix bayonets.

When we first started to do this exercise, it sounded like machine gun fire. This improved as we perfected our timing and got to the stage of the entire flight getting their bayonets to click home simultaneously on their rifles. I found the next stage of the drill a little frightening. I never really came to terms with marching at the slope arms with fixed bayonets. I could carry arms and march as well as any member of the flight. The problem was being of average height there was always a fifty fifty chance that I would have a shorter airman marching in front of me. On these occasions I found it quite horrific to see a bayonet bobbing about in front of me at eye level. Even now the thought of this experience leaves me cold. The final part of this aspect of training was bayonet combat training. It consisted of charging at the double with rifle and fixed bayonet extended forward at arms length. The objective was to plunge the bayonet into a straw filled dummy, twist the bayonet and then draw the rifle back with the bayonet still attached. The entire operation was carried out with the recruit under instructions to make horrendous screaming noises and imagine the dummy to be a Russian. I must confess that the operation was carried out with more enthusiasm if one imagined the dummy to be a DI.

Firearms – (The use of)

I have chosen to write this sub title in the true military fashion, back to front. After acquiring the skill to handle the Enfield 303 rifle as a drill object, the time came to learn the skill of using it as a weapon which was what it was for. In parallel with the 303 it would also be necessary to learn the complexities of the bren gun, (LMG). A rapid firing weapon which was designed with a prime objective of killing people. The instruction commenced in the lecture room and progressed to handling both weapons in the combat training area. This aspect of our training was under the direction of 'rock ape' combat instructors. The instruction on these weapons would eventually lead to each of us having to fire them in the controlled conditions of the firing range. Even when that stage was reached there would be a constraint put on what we could do as each man would be limited to twenty five rounds of live ammunition for his rifle; and thirty rounds (one magazine) for his LMG. This was due to the cost of the 303 ammunition. There is not a lot to say about the 303. It had been the mainstay weapon of the British Armed Services for many years, but by the mid 1950s was close to the end of its useful life, and was close to being replaced by a more up to date and technically sophisticated weapon. Nevertheless it was the weapon that was to be mastered by me and my contemporaries. The 303 was a joy to operate with its bolt action. It was easy to load with five rounds at a time from the bullet clip and a deft movement of the right fingers and thumb. This operation was of course perfected with practice. I felt comfortable with the 303 and enjoyed the experience of firing it on the range. Of the twenty five rounds of ammunition allocated to me the first five were used to warm up the gun and adjust its sights. The remaining twenty were fired in batches of five at four separate targets at a range of twenty five yards from the prone position. I was very proud when one of my targets was good enough to get me marksman classification. This was achieved by getting five consecutive shots within the inner and being able to cover them with a halfpenny. That was of course the old halfpenny, which was about the size of a two penny piece. I am certain I couldn't do this now with my double glazed specs.

The LMG was a different story, at least it was as far as I was concerned. It gave me absolutely no problems during basic weapon instruction. The trouble was when I had to eventually fire the ruddy thing. In this situation I didn't feel totally in control, in fact I was scared as I felt I was bouncing up and down on the butt of the gun, in time to its firing. Not a nice feeling. But I've got a little ahead of my tale, so I'll get back to writing about the basic instruction on the weapon. It was necessary to be able to dismantle and assemble the LMG rapidly even when blindfolded to simulate carrying out the operation in the dark. The gun had to be stripped in the precise sequence. The obvious first part to remove was the barrel as it had the weapon carrying handle attached to it. Next was the magazine as it stuck out and was untidy. The rest of the sequence could be remembered by silently thinking of a little poem that went thus – 'piss on the piston, but not on the bipod'. Which indicated the next piece to be removed was the piston assembly, followed by the butt and finally the bipod. I hope readers will excuse any minor errors in this section on weapon training, but memories do lapse a little with time. I have already dealt briefly with my disastrous performance when I fired the LMG on the range. Under the circumstances that brief description will suffice.

Our mastery of these weapons was to be finally put to the test in a night exercise. I was fortunate in not being allocated one of the limited number of bren guns available as they tended to get a bit heavy when carried over a distance. There was no ammunition, blank or live issued for the night's foray, this was fortunate as we had now reverted back to our ancient drill rifles, as opposed to the less, (note the word less) antiquated rifles we had used for firing on the range. The exercise turned out to be a monumental non event. The task of 'our side' was to defend from the enemy a hurricane lamp which was hanging from the top of a six foot pole on the side of a bracken covered Shropshire hillside. The enemy didn't materialize. My recollection of the exercise is of spending a totally sleepless night on a dew soaked, bracken covered Shropshire hillside in the company of one hurricane lamp and several recruits who were as equally pissed off as me. Yet again I'll finish a chapter with the classical quote of recruits, 'roll on demob'.

The Gas Chamber

Yes, you have read the subtitle correctly. This gas chamber was not as sophisticated as the type that existed in German concentration camps during the Second World War. To be perfectly truthful it resembled a garden shed of ample proportions and was located in the middle of a playing field at RAF Bridgnorth. We knew from our training programme that the gas chamber would play some part in our training. In spite of the training we had already received, we still had human weaknesses. One of these being the ability to totally ignore things that may prove to be unpleasant. That is until there was no alternative to face up to them. The day dawned when we reached the stage of having to face up to entering the gas chamber to learn the merits of the service issue respirator. When my respirator was issued it was obviously more technically advanced and heavier than the one I had been given as a child during the Second World War. After some very basic instruction on how to adjust and wear the respirator, it was off to the gas chamber in small groups. On reflection I believe the DIs objective was more motivated to getting their charges into the gas chamber than giving meaningful instructions on the respirator. So with minimum delay and no ceremony it was into the lion's den, sorry, gas chamber. Once inside we stood rather like a bunch of extras from a science fiction film. The DI stood in the middle of the circle of dejected humanity, as I am sure he had done on numerous other occasions and asked a question. 'Do you think there is gas in this room?' As I am sure had happened on numerous other occasions some silly beggar said 'no'. There of course always has to be one. I am sure the DI's eyes lit up at the response of the nameless illegitimate airman. The DI now had the cue to order 'remove respirators' and let's find out. He (the DI) of course pulled rank and kept his respirator on. It was obvious within seconds that the room was full of gas. But our discomfort was not to finish with a quick whiff of the stuff. The next bizarre order was to walk round the room singing, yes singing. Of all the songs we could have sung the order was to sing The Happy Wanderer. When it was judged that we had suffered the misery of the gas chamber sufficiently long enough, the door was opened and we emerged into that beautiful clear and sunny Shropshire air. We desperately needed to purge our bodies of the gas we had absorbed, this was achieved by doubling round the field until we dropped, of course we dropped by the NAAFI wagon which had put in a timely appearance. After the experience of the gas chamber there was no doubt in anybodies mind of the importance of keeping our respirators serviced and to hand for use within seconds should it be necessary.

Medicals, Jabs and Allied Unpleasantaries.

There seemed to be a conspiracy amongst medical personnel at no. seven S of R T that it was their God given role in life to inflict the maximum of discomfort on recruits in their charge. The human body is a wonderful thing, but is extremely vulnerable due to the number of orifices it is blessed with. Some more obvious than others.

The medical personnel seemed to delight in examining one or more of these orifices at frequent intervals, very often to the discomfort and embarrassment of recruits. In addition to these frequent examinations of earholes, noseholes etc., they also appeared to get a sadistic pleasure from sticking needles into recruits to give them immunity from little known unpleasant diseases. Whenever the medical personnel carried out the aforementioned unpleasantaries they went to considerable trouble to try and reassure recruits it was for their own good. What a monumental load of bull. The examination that seemed to be the most frequent was the FFI, (short arm inspection). It was also the inspection that prompted the most discussion. The tale I heard from many old sweats about a particular FFI went thus. The MO was walking along a line of servicemen who had their trousers at the trail. He stopped in front of a particularly 'big' man, lifted a part of this man's anatomy with his swagger stick, and remarked, 'Your a fine fellow, I bet that's been in a few nests?' To which the man replied, 'Yes sir, but it's the first time it's been on a perch'. Surely this must constitute one of the classic of line shoots.

I have written earlier in this chapter about jabs. Whilst not a very pleasant thing to have they were totally necessary for the protection of service personnel from some of the terrible diseases that existed in some of the foreign holes in which we may well have to go to for the purpose of serving Queen and Country. The main problem I personally experienced on the day I had my jabs was not as a result of action by medical personnel, but by the bloody minded actions of a Corporal DI, whom I can best describe as a prat of the first order. We lined up and received our 'basic' jabs, which to the best of my recollection totalled four. It was a boiling hot August afternoon. It was, at this point, that our moronic Corporal DI decided it would be a good idea to have us run round the sports field to get the vaccine circulating. The result was disastrous, as the combination of heat, exercise and jabs caused several recruits to pass out, and many more to feel unwell. The result was a full sick bay and curtailment of the remainder of the day's training programme. If that particular DI had done that amount of harm to an enemy, he would have got a medal.

Blood Donors

The blood transfusion unit paid regular visits to 7S of R.T. as they did to all military establishments, which at that time must have been a major source of donors. The DI's used a considerable amount of intimidation to obtain 'volunteers' to give blood. As a result of giving blood on that occasion I became a regular donor for many years and certainly felt better for having made this humble contribution for the benefit of my fellow beings.

Reliability and Initiative Training

This phase of training was based on a theory that had its origin in pure logic, so it had to be good. It was assumed that most recruits came to the service with at least a degree of reasoning power and intelligence. The Whitehall warriors in their wisdom decided that efforts should be made to ensure that these qualities of the recruits should not be lost. It was assumed that this may happen as a result of recruits being bawled at and chased from breakfast to supper time by moronic persons of very limited intelligence. Reliability and initiative training was introduced with the objective of encouraging recruits to use their brains and organising skills in performing competitive tasks in small groups. This particular training took up about four hours per week, until it reached its climax with a three day camp during the last few days of week six of square bashing. For the purpose of this aspect of training was to be camping at its most primitive with no tents or sleeping bags. We did however have the basics, namely, a service issue cape, which was designed and intended to double as a ground sheet. In addition we each had two blankets, plus one ball of string between each six man team. Each day started with tasks being given to each team. The most important of these being the map reference and time that the rendezvous had to be made with the ration wagon. More than fifteen minutes late meant six hungry team members, so there was an incentive to succeed. I must admit that I got a lot of pleasure from those few days as I was an outdoor person, the experience was not as alien to me as it was to some of my colleagues. On return to Bridgnorth camp the first task was a hot bath. I must admit that I felt better after it, as for the three days of the camp my personal washing had been limited to a quick cat lick in any convenient stream.

Civilian Personnel and Fatigues

A double title, but as you read it will become apparent that there is a connection. I accept that it is remote. Nevertheless, it is there. One of the lectures during the middle period of training was on the complexities of running an organisation the size of the RAF. To emphasise this point we were told that at some point in our training we would gain first hand experience of having to operate the organisation from the sharp end. This was to be achieved by doing a three day stint of fatigues on menial tasks. I suppose this had some logic as it utilised cheap captive labour. The thing that seemed grossly unfair, was that fatigues was normally used as a form of punishment for those of our number who had erred, on this occasion even the 'good guys' were to be lumbered.

The business of the three days of fatigues did have a certain ring of logic, that is of course the distorted logic of some of the decision makers. A large number of the people running the RAF at that time, (I can't comment on how it is now), had very blinkered views coupled with an inbred openly hostility to all people who were not members of their somewhat limited social world, but thats life.

For my sins the DI sent me to the airmen's mess for my three days of organisational enlightenment (fatigues). Not for me the task of preparing some gastronomical delight for my fellow recruits. Not even 'spud bashing' or washing up; thank goodness. It was at least some consolation that the RAF had now mechanised these two unpleasant tasks.

My main task in the mess was to assist with the dishing out of food at meal times, hardly the best of jobs to develop my organisational skills. It was the tasks I had between meal times that I found the most difficult to accept. But like any good and loyal serviceman, accept them I did, without query. I don't even query them now, but I do criticise them and the persons involved in their perpetration. The service authorities employed large numbers of civilian personnel to carry out non military duties on the station. Several of these civilians were employed on domestic duties in the airmans mess. During my period of fatigues in the mess it became obvious that some DIs received favourable treatment in the mess for certain considerations. One of these considerations was allocation of fatigues party members to carry out some of the civilian personnel's tasks. From my personal observations I would sum up, a small minority of RAF Bridgnorth's civilian staff as 'idle'.

Square Bashing Trivia

(Including – Laundry, Haircuts, Passes, Fire & Security Picket and The Great Tea Myth).

Laundry

As you can well imagine many of our clothes, (particularly 'woollen' socks) got in a disgusting state, as a result of our physical activities and the hot weather. A method existed which allowed us to send items of clothing to the laundry, although I must admit that I was totally bemused by the way some people interpreted the instructions. The laundry card was about the size of an average envelope. On it was printed details of the items of clothing that could be sent for laundering. It was therefore only necessary to identify on the card, the items actually being sent. It was permitted to send twelve items each week. This is the point at which the problems started. The moronic DI's decided that this meant that each one of us must send twelve items to the laundry. Their logic was such that if any recruit did not have twelve dirty items to have laundered he had to make the number up with clean items. I think my readers will agree this was strange reasoning, even for morons. The most disturbing factor is of course these decisions were made by those entrusted with the training of others.

Haircuts

There is no doubt that the hairdressing facility at square bashing camps throughout the United Kingdom created considerable local employment. It was necessary for recruits to have a 'trim' about once a week in order to maintain the state of semi baldness that was demanded of them. This frequency was often reduced as a result of action by the DIs. At times they would detail recruits to get a haircut, usually in groups of thirteen, (twelve for the barber, one for the DI). It was suggested that when this happened it was always on the day before pay parade if the particular DI didn't have any beer money. This is an interesting theory, I must state it is only an unsubstantiated theory. That is of course unless any of you know otherwise.

Passes

There must have been hundreds of different ones in existence, but my concern was confined to a mere three. Namely my own '1250', any '295' that chanced to come my way and whilst at Bridgnorth my permanent pass. The permanent pass was only applicable to me whilst I was at square bashing, the other two retained their importance throughout my service career. Permanent passes were housed in the flight office and had to be collected before any recruit was permitted to leave camp. The permanent pass, together with the holder's 1250 had to be shown to the duty snowdrop at the camp gate before the holder was allowed out. The pass allowed the recruit to be out of camp until 23.59 hours, but never over night. On return to camp the pass and 1250 had to be shown to regain entry via the main gate, the alternative was to enter over the three foot threadbare hedge at the rear of the camp. The latter route was favoured by those who had a drop too much of the local brew and considered it best to avoid the snowdrops. The most important thing was to have the pass back in the flight office by 23.59 hours as failure to do this rendered the offender liable to have to face the serious charge of being AWOL. To the best of my knowledge the only exception to the 23.59 hours rule was if the offender was on officially service sponsored transport which had suffered an unforeseeable delay. It was quite normal for the flight duty DI to carry out a bed check shortly after 23.59 hours as recruits had been known to nip out over the hedge to keep dates or just bug the system. The ones most likely to do this would be recruits who had been confined to barracks and had their passes suspended.

Fire and Security Picket

This was a very unglamorous night time duty. Especially as it was carried out after a hard day's training, (all days of training were hard at square bashing camp). I did this particular duty twice whilst I was at RAF Bridgnorth. At the start of the duty the picket members reported to the guard room or fire section, complete with bedding. The night's duties would then be handed out based on a two hours on and two hours off basis. The duty was from dusk to dawn and was carried out by members of the picket operating in pairs. When on duty a pair of men would patrol the perimeter of the camp and make a special point of inspecting all the military installations for security and possible unauthorised intruders. This of course was supposed to allow all the residents to sleep safely in their beds. It is worthy of note that the camp was huge, the installations were numerous and well spread out. There was a large armoury full of weapons and ammunition. The threat from the IRA and similar terrorist organisations was as real then as it is now. Never mind, residents of the camp could sleep well knowing that throughout the night they were protected by at least two inexperienced recruits who had been well armed with a pick axe handle and whistle each.

The Great Tea Myth

AUTHOR'S NOTE – Many old sweats may well be enraged by me choosing to write on this particular subject in a section that deals with what I personally consider trivia. I agree that the particular aspect of my writing is on what was, and probably still is, highly emotive. I decided that as I am the writer, it is up to me to make the rules. Therefore as what I shall write on the subject will be purely speculation and inconclusive with no hope of closing the long running debate, I have no option other than to treat the subject as trivia . . .

Oh how this subject was and probably still is debated. Its mere mention was as controversial as would be the sighting of a pregnant nun. I think that I have perhaps illustrated by just how the effect the tea myth, sorry, the great tea myth could and did have on people. I am getting ahead of myself so I'll try to explain, although even greater souls than I have been baffled by the myth over many years.

Historically the myth should be treated as two fold as it was/is alleged to apply to/have applied to tea served both in the airmens mess and the NAAFI. There was a rumour running rife that the tea served to those below the rank of Sergeant contained an additive that was supposed to curtail the drinker's sexual urges. There was always considerable discussion and doubt, either way, as to the authenticity of this rumour. Factually there always appeared to be a large number of healthy children around the married quarters of every station at which I served. In addition to this my eldest daughter was born some three months after my demobilisation from the RAF in 1957. So was it a myth or not?

Did it or didn't it have an additive?

Or was it a monumental line shoot that was kept going by rumour and doubt?

Whatever the truth, who would believe it? I suggest, very few.

RAF BRIDGNORTH – SUMMER 1955

The author is the eighth from the left, in the third row from the rear.

Chapter 10

ASPECTS OF SQUARE BASHING – THE FINALE – WEEKS SEVEN AND EIGHT

At last, this was it, a member of the Senior Flight. I must confess that it was at times a goal that seemed unattainable, but my colleagues (most of them) and I made it. Two more weeks to go and a step closer to the real airforce. As, during the earlier weeks of square bashing, many things would happen that would affect our service careers and the pace of training would certainly not slow down. As members of the senior flight we were looked on with awe by lesser recruits as we had survived and gone through what they still had to face up to. Our mode of dress also distinguished as the Senior Flight as we wore our peaked caps on camp, even when in shirt sleeve order. The final act in the saga would be the passing out parade which would be attended by sundry civilians, such as wives, girl friends, parents and in a few cases mistresses, more about the passing out parade later. I'll deal briefly with each of the events of those last memorable two weeks at RAF Bridgnorth. There was still a lot more drill to be done in preparation for the drill test, at which we would have to show our ability in front of the reviewing officers. The showing at drill test would not only determine the top group in the flight, but would also be a deciding factor as to our ability to be on the passing out parade. The drill test was a full dress rehearsal for the passing out ceremony and of course there was the constant threat of being deflighted two weeks if anybody dared to not give of their best. This threat in itself was sufficient incentive to try hard. The drill test was duly taken and my section came out with top marks and the drill trophy. It was about this time that I made my first flight in the RAF, it was infact my first ever flight as flying for the masses was a novelty at that time. Although I was to ultimately do a considerable amount of flying in the airforce, my first flight was still a bit special. To the best of my recollection it was from RAF Cosford and was in a very aged Avro Anson. I later came across this type of aircraft on several occasions in connection with my work on aero engines.

Battle of Britain week occurred during this last period at Bridgnorth. The station had been invited to provide a contingent of men to join the parade in the neighbouring town of Stourbridge. It was logical that this task should fall to the Senior Flight. On the appropriate Sunday morning we dutifully paraded, complete with white gloves and webbing belts. We were spared having to carry rifles and fixed bayonets as the station, (fortunately) did not hold the freedom of entry to the town. We paraded behind a band who performed in a manner that led me to believe that they had consumed a considerable amount of alcohol before they paraded. In fact several of the musicians appeared to be 'pissed'. The RAF contingent was the only service group in the parade, which was largely made up of members of youth organisations and other sundry obscure civilian organisations. It fell to us to provided the necessary swank to uphold the good name of the British Armed Service. I believe we succeeded. As we came to attention we slammed our well studded boots to the ground so hard that the noise made several onlookers visibly jump. I believe that several of these startled civilians would have needed to change items of their underwear after our efforts. Need I explain further?

Another important event during that last two week period was the trade selection list. The outcome of this would determine what the RAF future would be for each of us. As a fully qualified motor engineer with a City and Guilds qualification, I had indicated that I would like to spend my service career in motor transport. This appeared to be the most sensible, based on pure logic. But of course

I had still not learned that the armchair warriors controlling the RAF had little or no understanding of logic. Their principle of logic appeared to be to look at the obvious and then do the opposite. This seems to have a similarity with the Civil Service and politicians.

One fear that I did have was that I would be made a Snowdrop as I had gained some police experience as a Special Constable prior to being called up. When I saw the trade list, I got a surprise, not an unpleasant one. I had not got my first choice but was to train as an engine mechanic. The engines being aero engines of the piston type, not turbines. I would have to spend twelve weeks at RAF technical training unit before I was let loose on an operational aircraft. I consoled myself that when I would eventually return to my civilian employment in the experimental department at a commercial vehicle manufacturers I may well have considerable additional useful experience.

As the day of the passing out parade drew nearer there was a last visit to the station tailor for final uniform adjustments. Considerable time was spent of bulling up the toe caps of boots for the big day. Mary was going to have a day off work and with my parents would attend the parade, this meant a lot to me. Pass out day finally came. There was much to do and not a lot of time to do it. Bedding had to be handed in, kit bags had to be packed as we would be leaving RAF Bridgnorth immediately after the parade. There was no chance to welcome our visitors before the parade, the station personnel met them at the gate and escorted them to their appointed places to watch the parade. The members of my flight paraded outside our billet for the last time for an inspection before marching onto the parade ground. A Sergeant DI not only carried out the inspection, he also carried a duster with which to flick the odd bit of dust off an airmans boots or buttons, what a load of bull. We then fixed bayonets and with rifles at the slope marched onto the parade ground. The parade went well and I was later assured by the onlookers that the occasion was impressive. We marched off the parade ground straight to the armoury to hand in our rifles and bayonets. It was then back to the billet for the last time, purely to collect kit. It was not necessary for me to leave RAF Bridgnorth in full marching order, as I had arrived, so all my webbing was packed in my kit bag. I took my leave of RAF Bridgnorth on that bright September day in 1955. I was off home with Mary armed with a seven day leave pass and instructions to report to the RAF Weeton (Lancashire) school of technical training at the end of my leave.

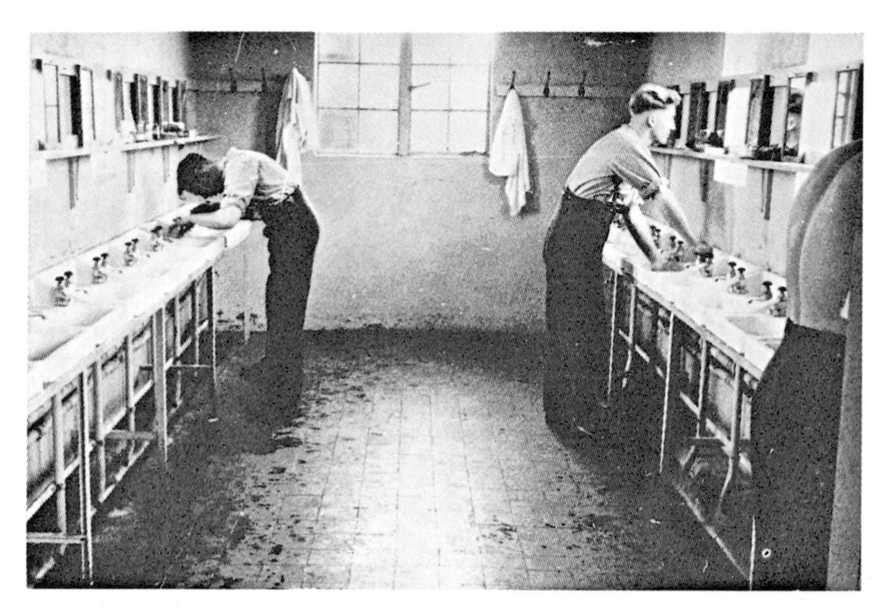

A Bridgnorth Ablution – one of the better ones.

CHAPTER 11

ROYAL AIR FORCE WEETON

My post square bashing leave was over and I was about to take my next step towards the real airforce. The airforce of aeroplanes and people associated with them. That was my hope when on the appointed day, I presented myself, (complete with packed kit bag) at the gates of number eight school of technical training. This was the posh or official title of RAF Weeton, near Blackpool, Lancashire. Blackpool, the town whose name was dreaded by an earlier generation of airmen, who during the early days of World War Two had done their basic training on the beach and promenade of that northern seaside town. On reflection their dread was perhaps not so much of Blackpool as of the world renowned landladies of that town, as most of those hapless airmen were billeted in the boarding houses which were owned and run by these ladies whom for many years had provided valuable ammunition for variety theatre comedians.

So I'd arrived at RAF Weeton. I must admit that prior to receiving my orders to report there, I'd never heard of the ruddy place, I'd even been unable to find it on the map. It was my third station in less than three months as an airman. Weeton was without doubt the largest RAF station that I had seen to date. It was not only home of the aero engine training school, but also housed the RAF driving school and an area hospital of considerable size and repute. I arrived there with the title of 'AC2 U/T engine mech. (P)', which in service terms put me one step, (a very small step), above the lowest form of life in the RAF. I would of course have the chance of advancement in the service. Any advancement would be related to how well I did on my engine course, allied to my conduct, (keeping my nose clean). It was suggested in the services at that time (and probably still is), that good conduct was achieved by being crafty, (sorry), clever enough as not to allow those in authority to become aware of one's lapses, (crimes). This bears a strange similarity to the civilian system, doesn't it? But back to the start of my Weeton experience. I was welcomed, (for want of a better word) by an old school Admin Flight Sergeant. He was a Welshman who had built up a reputation as a hard beggar. What a load of rubbish. This hardness was a facade and as my colleagues and I got to know him better, he proved to be one of the most helpful and understanding people with whom I came into contact during my National Service. When sufficient of us were mustered in the flight office it was time for our Welsh Flight Sergeant to give verse to his well practised spiel, which over the years he had no doubt delivered on hundreds of occasions. One part of this spiel was directed in particular at the unworldly members of the gathering. To the best of my recollection it went thus. 'This camp is close to an oversized fishing village which is known as Blackpool. Blackpool has an area known as the golden mile. The golden mile is said to be paved with gold. If this is the case, the gold has come from the pockets of unsuspecting young persons, such as some of you shower, so beware'. He possibly expressed himself in slightly more 'flowery' terms than I have, but my memory is slightly fogged after almost forty years. There is little doubt that he gave his message in a way that was well understood. Even by the most naive of his captive audience. I was allocated a billet and proceeded to it via the bedding stores. The accommodation at Weeton was in the usual service style wooden huts. The huts at Weeton were mostly in an advanced state of disrepair and general knackerisation. There was however a refurbishment programme in progress, but it was obvious that huts were deteriorating faster than they could be codged up. Each hut provided a home for about twenty airmen. The method of heating was by means of two ancient solid fuel, cast iron stoves. Very inefficient in the north country winter, even stoked up until they became red hot, but more of that later.

So this was it, my home for the next twelve weeks, (it would in fact be fourteen weeks due to training being curtailed for Christmas and then having to wait for a posting). As day one came to a close, after a game of snooker and a cup of NAAFI tea, Ugh, I came to the conclusion that Weeton may not be too bad. The station regime was fairly liberal and geared to technical matters rather than the endless bull of Bridgnorth.

Mary (centre) with her sister and friends from work, on a visit to Blackpool during my time at RAF Weeton.

CHAPTER 12

WEETON - THE FIRST FULL DAY

This was to be a very casual and civilised introduction of what was in store. Some of the staff instructors went briefly through the technicalities of the engine course content with us. It was obvious that the course would not only cover engines, but would deal in depth with propellers, ancillary service systems, aircraft ground handling and ground testing of engines. There would be two courses running in parallel. One to cover mechanics (T), turbine - (jet). The other being for mechanics (P), piston. This was my course which would cover inline and radial engines of sleeve valve and poppet valve types. With all the allied systems to be learned it was obvious that the training was going to be intense, but informative and enjoyable. The training was divided into specific phases of one and two week's duration. It was necessary to take an exam at the end of each phase before being permitted to move on to the next. A failure meant having to repeat the failed phase. Each trainee was permitted a maximum of one failure. A second failure would result in being remustered into some menial and generally unpleasant job. So there was a substantial incentive to succeed, this was further endorsed by the possibility of promotion in one's trade, with its allied financial reward. The talk on our course content was followed by a brief conducted tour of the training hangars and lecture rooms. This tour was particularly informative as it would ultimately save considerable time as we moved from one installation to another for different aspects of the course. As well as lectures and practical work we would be given adequate time for physical recreation of a personal choice. In addition there would be compulsory sessions of PT and a weekly Padre's hour. During the conducted tour I took note of the area in general. It was obvious from the angle of which the trees and bushes grew that the area had a strong prevailing wind from the sea. This assumption proved true as winter came. Blackpool Tower was just visible on the horizon across that particularly bleak and uninviting Lancashire countryside. I later realised just how bleak and miserable the area was as winter came.

Apart from the activities already mentioned there would be very little restriction on how I used my off duty time. It was compulsory to attend church parade on one's first Sunday at Weeton. After that weekends would be free from noon on Saturday until 23.59 hours on Sunday. It was also permitted to wear civilian clothes when not on duty. It looked as if life at Weeton would be a step towards normality after the period of conditioning during square bashing.

CHAPTER 13

ENGINE MECHANICS COURSE (P)

To explain the (P) after the title. There were two types of mechanics. P for piston engine and T for turbine (jet) engines. Both courses ran in parallel with the necessary course content variations to suit the different types of engines. The piston engine training was divided into specific phases of one or two week's duration each. The length of each phase was determined by the volume and complexity of its content. The phase work would be carried out in lecture rooms, workshops, hangars with a certain amount out of doors. Weeton had never been an operational station for flying, but had several large hangars which over the years had been used to house equipment associated with the station's various training activities. I find it impossible to be precise as to each phase after the passage of so many years but what follows is a brief run down of my engineering training as I recall it.

The first training phase was in the fitting workshop and was designed to teach students the basic use of hand tools. Many of the course members had no experience of working with their hands, some did however have an inbred aversion to getting their hands dirty. With the practical and 'verbal' encouragement of the instructors this aversion was short lived.

This first phase caused me no problems as the work involved was allied to what I was familiar with as an engineer. Even the filed test pieces were similar to tests I had done as an apprentice.

The next phase was basic engines. The engines used would be De Havilland four and six cylinder in line gipsy engines. Although I was familiar with many petrol and diesel engines my previous experience was confined to vehicle, marine and industrial engines. Although there was some similarity with aero engines and vehicle engines there was a tremendous difference in the design and engineering applications between the two. Some of the obvious differences being that the gipsy engines had the crankshaft above the cylinders, in effect upside down in relation to a vehicle engine. The gipsy engines were also air cooled and had their tappets adjusted when cold, unlike the majority of vehicle engines which had their tappets adjusted when hot. It was obvious from the start of this phase that whilst I was experienced and well qualified on vehicles and their engines I was now part of a new ball game and would have to restart from scratch. So after my easy start on phase one in the workshop I was now on a par with the rest of my colleagues. Not a bad thing. One particular lecture caused amusement, strange as it was about the magneto. Hardly an amusing subject so I'll need to explain. The Corporal Instructor asked for a volunteer to assist him in demonstrating the mag. One naive and not very bright student offered his services. The Instructor, with much mock theatricals accepted the offer of help from the poor hapless soul. The instructor produced a small magneto which had been stripped of all its external wires, which of course left several finger size orifices. The instructor asked his unsuspecting assistant to put his little fingers in two of the orifices on opposite sides of the mag., thus steadying the mag, which was on the table. When the hapless helper had complied, the Instructor with a sadistic self satisfied smirk on his face gave the magneto a quick turn. The result to say the least was 'electric'. The hapless helper broke the record for a standing vertical jump, I also suspect he was in desperate need of clean underpants. With further mock theatricals our sadistic Instructor thanked his assistant for his help in teaching his colleagues respect for magnetos.

The basic engine phase continued in a progressive routine way with no further incidents which are worthy of special note. I was delighted to pass this phase, which enabled me to move forward in my training, but there was still a long way to go as the half way stage had not yet been reached. Part of the training course was devoted to aspects of an engine mechanic's duties which were devoted to aircraft in general as opposed to engines. It was necessary in times of adverse weather conditions to be able to secure parked aircraft safely. This could be achieved by parking into wind or even roping the aircraft to the ground. It was necessary to be able to visually direct, (Marshal) taxiing aircraft by means of internationally recognised signals. This operation was carried out in darkness with the use of hand held illuminated wands. Engine mechanics also, at times, became the extra pair of hands to other tradesmen on the team when assistance was required. This arrangement was reciprocal with all tradesmen and led to very flexible demarcation lines within the service team. With the industrial strife of the 1950s, industry could have learned a lot from the service methods.

This phase also dealt in some depth with the use of specialist ground equipment. Many items that would ultimately be used by my fellow students and I on a daily basis in connection with our work. This equipment consisted of - starter trolleys, generators, flood lights, aircraft towing attachments for use with tractors, plus many more items too numerous to mention, but all directly involved with the ground handling of aircraft. I actually got near an aircraft during this phase. It was a very ancient Avro Anson. We turned it into imaginary winds, tied it down, chocked it and unchocked it, positioned an imaginary bowser to refuel it. Infact, did everything that the limited space in the hangar allowed, this excluded actually running the engines. Although our training was to eventually cover the theory of this, none of us would actually run an engine until we reached an operational squadron. Although the Annie, (Anson) and some of the equipment we used in this phase was ancient it was sufficiently good enough for us to get familiar with the type of equipment that was in daily squadron use.

One training phase was devoted entirely to paperwork. It must be appreciated that an organisation as vast and as complex as the RAF in the 1950s, not only needed a system of accurate records of all service of its aircraft and equipment. There was also the political implication that as it was funded entirely by tax payers' money very many people needed to know how the money was being used. Good record keeping was essential for many reasons and it would have been morally wrong not to teach mechanics what was expected and demanded of them in respect of written records. There was also the other aspect of teaching a person to use manuals and text books to obtain information that it was necessary for them to have to do a job correctly. This not only applied to how the work should be done, but the right way to obtain the necessary parts to carry out the task. During one of the phases of training considerable time was spent on the subject of AGS parts and their importance. It had to be realised that whatever any of us had learned and done in civilian life, it was necessary to learn and adapt to the military working environment, and more especially the systems and rules that applied. Even in peace time this demanded total commitment and dedication. When working on aircraft, irrespective of trade, an error of judgement or minor lapse of concentration could be disastrous for many people. This illustrates why trade training was taken so seriously, even on aspects that appeared trivial. Another thing I learned that was to be very useful when I joined a Squadron was how to swing a prop to start an engine. It was of the utmost importance to carry out this particular operation according to the book as even a minor error in the execution of this particular operation may at least cause injury, or more seriously could be fatal. Propellers made up a full phase of training. The range covered in training varied from the simple traditional fixed pitch types as used on Chipmunks and Tiger Moths, to the large multi bladed variable pitch props as used on transport planes. I was amazed when I got involved in the technicalities of props by the number of component parts in their construction and operational systems. The interrelated controls between engine speed and prop pitch. The fact that the prop operated directly from the engine made it an important aspect of the mechanic's work. I was now in sight of the final phase of my engine course. Just two weeks left to learn a little about two more engines before having to take my final trade test. The engines to be covered in advanced engines phase were:

1. The Bristol Hercules fourteen cylinder, sleeve valved, air cooled, radial engine. Not only did this engine have the most complicated valve timing gears I had ever seen, (or have since seen). It also had a supercharger, twin magnetos and two sparking plugs per cylinder, making a total of twenty eight plugs per engine. I was later to find out how cold it could be to do a plug change at a windy airfield in the middle of winter.

2. The Rolls Royce Merlin liquid cooled 'V' engine. This engine had a pedigree second to none. During World War Two it had been the chosen power unit of the Spitfire, Hurricane and Lancaster plus several revered British aircraft. In anybody's language that has to be a true top drawer pedigree.

This particular phase was intense, as it was the culmination of the entire course. It was the point at which the entire training programme fitted together and had some meaning. The phase culminated with the final exam of the course. I was delighted when I got the news that I had passed the exam and once it became official by appearing on PROs I would be a fully fledged AC1 engine mech (P).

With friends at RAF Weeton – Winter 1955

CHAPTER 14

WEETON MISCELLANY

Transit

When my course finished I was destined to be in the transit flight for about one week. During this time various faceless desk pilots, at numerous locations, would be working frantically to determine how I would spend my service career. They would be charged with many monumental tasks such as promoting me (on paper) from AC2 to AC1, arranging to increase my pay by a few pence per day. However, the biggest worry for me was that one of those faceless pen pushing odd bods would determine my posting. At that time more than fifty percent of National Servicemen finished up overseas. As well as European postings many went to the Middle or Far East. So it was going to be a waiting game for about a week before my destiny was known. As a member of the transit flight I had to do some work that would contribute to the running of the station. My allotted tasks were in the transit flight mess, this was without doubt one of the cushiest numbers an airman could have. The work consisted of assisting on the servery at breakfast time. Spending the morning on general mess duties, including vegetable preparation. After assisting on the servery at lunch time and having my own lunch, I was then free until I worked on the servery for about one hour at tea time. Not a bad work routine for a transit wallah. As an added bonus not only was the Sergeant in charge of the mess an extremely competent chef, he was also a gentleman who got the best from his full time staff and temporary helpers by treating them with dignity. I was and still am a person who enjoys his food, so the mess job was a perk more than a chore. One particular lunch time I saw a large serving tray full of what I assumed was a particularly thick, rich, brown stew. It was garnished with an intricate pattern of boiled rice, which in turn was topped with slices of hard boiled egg. When the time came for the helpers to eat I served myself a substantial helping of this brown stew. I had in fact had my first taste of curry, a very potent one. I have since acquired a taste for curry. But I shall never forget my first taste of this Eastern delight. It was an enlightening experience.

Weekends

With the exception of two, I spent part of each weekend at home, the exceptions being compulsory church parade attendance and the other much happier occasion when Mary and several of her friends came to Blackpool on a works outing to see the illuminations. The weekends on which I got home were on a thirty six hour leave pass which was operative from noon on Saturday until 23.59 hours on Sunday. The Blackpool/Birmingham return train fare at that time was £1-5-0 (£1.25). I could not afford that from my service pay, so I normally hitchhiked home on Saturday afternoon and returned to camp by train on Sunday evening. I became a very proficient hitch-hiker and reckoned to be home by 4.00 p.m. Earlier than I could do the journey by train and bus. Good going as the journey was made pre motorway.

One of my fellow course students came from Stratford on Avon, and owned a motor cycle. On one occasion he offered me a lift home as a pillion passenger. I accepted as it provided a direct means of transport home for the weekend. He warned me that I would need to dress up to suit the weather as we were now well into winter. Following his advice I put on as many layers of clothes as I could and finished off by covering the lot with my RAF greatcoat. This was before skid lids became compulsory or fashionable so my head gear was my service flat cap, with of course the chinstrap in place to prevent my hat blowing away, (I was going to say 'to prevent my hat blowing off' but I thought that terminology was perhaps open to misinterpretation). We set out at midday on a cold Saturday for the Midlands and home. By the time we got a few miles down the road to Preston I felt cold. We got a little further to Wigan and I was feeling colder than I had ever felt before. The next town we came to was Warrington, I was now paralysed by the cold but managed to summon up the effort necessary to tap my companion on the shoulder as a signal that I wanted him to stop. When he stopped I managed to get off his machine, to this day I still don't know how I managed to do so.

I courteously thanked him for the lift to that point and proceeded to complete my journey by the well tried and proven hitchhiking method. Since that day I have never been on a motor cycle or had any desire to own one, ride one or be remotely associated with one.

During weekends at home we watched a little television. On Sunday afternoons the popular American situation comedy 'I married Joan' was screened. The end of the programme was a signal that it was time to have tea prior to Mary and I travelling into Birmingham for me to catch a train from New Street Station for the journey back to camp. The station was always bustling on Sunday evenings with service personnel on the move to their various locations after their weekend leave. I had to get a Blackpool train to Kirkham as Weeton did not have a railway station, but Kirkham was only a couple of miles away. The journey took about three hours and was via Crewe.

Fortunately on most occasions I was spared the task of having to change at the well known junction that had been the butt of so many comedians' jokes over the years. The trains I travelled on at that time were of the good and faithful steam variety. I have been a life long enthusiast of steam and during some of those Sunday night trips I travelled on trains that were hauled by what had been some of the great locomotives of the LMS. But alas the circumstances in which I made these weekly journeys gave me little or no pleasure. As the train neared Kirkham, the Weeton airmen would cram the carriage doorways ready to leap off the train when it stopped and be first in the dash off the platform and out of the station. Weeton camp was about two miles from the railway station and served by a bus service, of sorts. The quickest way to cover those couple of miles of unlit and winding Lancashire lanes was by hire car/taxi. These hire cars were mostly aged Austin Sixteens which were driven by some of the RAF driving instructors from Weeton who earned a bit of extra cash by moonlighting as hire car drivers. If five or six of us squeezed into one of these cars it only cost 1/6 (7 ½p) each, it only cost 6d (2 ½p) by bus, but the extra was well worth it. I hope this has explained the urge to get off the train and out of the station quickly. Being at the front of the dash had several advantages such as:

1. Being in one of the cars on its first trip to Weeton, they had to make several journeys to transport all those who needed to get to the camp.
2. Being among the first back at the camp gates meant being at the front of the queue to purchase a hot meat and potato pie from the food vender who was there each evening.
3. It was then back to the billet to nab one of the limited seats close to a stove, and enjoy the hot supper whilst listening to 'Record round up' on the radio. This particular programme was the forerunner to today's hit parade and was well presented by Jack Jackson assisted by the sound effects of Tiddles.

Weeton Winter

I have experienced many cold winters during my fifty plus years in this world. What made the winter of 1955/56 so particularly miserable was the fact that I had no option but to spend most of it at RAF Weeton. The camp was located in what must be one of the most inhospitable corners of Lancashire, over many years the Whitehall warriors seemed to have perfected the technique of locating service establishments in such places. The wooden billets were heated by very ancient cast iron stoves, two stoves per hut. These stoves were normally fuelled, (note normally) by coke of which the ration was one bucket full, per stove, per day. There was no chance of fiddling this modest ration as all types of fuel were contained in a secured compound. There was an unofficial and highly irregular salvation which was turned to in desperation in the fight to keep warm. On reflection the persons who resorted to these desperate methods may well have faced serious charges if they had been caught. I will refrain from writing down any names, or indeed to making any admissions. There was a major billet refurbishment programme in progress, this was necessary as many of Weeton billets were in a state of near collapse. As fast as the contractors replaced wood in particular billets on which they were employed some of the new wood, together with vast quantities of old wood disappeared during the hours of darkness. I have in fact seen billets practically disappear over night. I can personally vouch that the disappearing timber contributed in a small way to the comfort and well being of some very brassed off airmen, who at least had a fire to sit by. I have often wondered if the refurbishment of the Weeton billets was ever completed?

Postings

Part way through this period we were informed that our postings had come through. All the newly qualified engine mechanics, both piston and turbine, assembled in one of the lecture rooms to receive the tidings. Pleasant or otherwise. In all there were about sixty of us waiting for some desk bound wingless wonder to experience his moment of glory as he read out a list of what the future held for his audience of sixty apprehensive airmen. There was total silence in the room, this was the signal for the immature and squeaky voiced officer to start reading out the postings list. As he progressed all the postings seemed to be overseas. Places such as Aden, Cyprus, Singapore, Hong Kong and several others that must have been little more than disease and fly infested jungle clearings that the politicians considered should have a British presence for the purpose of showing the flag. When the list had passed the half way mark my name had not been called, it was also disturbing that neither had anybody to that point received a home posting. To say I was now in a nervous state would be a gross understatement, to use the appropriate service language, it would be fair to say I was near to having kittens. The list went on, still without any news for me, and still all overseas postings. At long last my name, and relief as he read out my posting. Abingdon on Thames, Berkshire (it has since become Oxfordshire). Not only had I got a home posting, I'd got one within seventy miles of home, out of all sixty of us only four had home postings, all to Abingdon. Not only was Abingdon fairly close to home, it was adjacent to the A34 trunk road which passed within a few miles of my home. The airmen with overseas postings were to go home immediately for seven days embarkation leave, prior to departing to their far flung destinations. Those of us with home postings would have to remain on transit flight for a few more days until our travelling instructions came through. During those few days I had time to think how lucky I was with my posting. Not only would I be one hundred and fifty miles south, which would take me well away from the north country winter, I would be considerably closer to home. The last couple of points, whilst of some consolation, didn't alter the fact that I would still have rather been a civilian.

Recreation - (Constructive, Formal, Informal)

As my time at Weeton was late Autumn and Winter my activities (other than studying) were largely dictated by the weather. This at least maintained any element of typical British behaviour. Each week one complete afternoon had to be devoted to participating in an approved recreational activity. The word approved introduced an immediate limitation on what one could do. At the time I was an enthusiastic recreational ice skater and there was a rink in Blackpool. I was on occasions lucky enough to get one of the limited concessionary entry tickets to the rink, as I had my own skates it was possible to have an afternoon's skating at a reasonable price. On the weeks I was unable to go to the ice rink I went on the cross country run. I had a very valid and logical reason for choosing this particular activity.

The ablution facilities at Weeton were at best, poor and at worst primitive. They were in premises of corrugated iron construction which housed showers, baths, wash basins and bogs. They had a limited (very limited) supply of hot water and no heating. They were in fact crude in the extreme. By going on the cross country run, which was little more than a pleasant jog of about five miles, it was possible to be in the first few people to shower whilst there was hot water available. Whereas those poor souls that had taken part in activities of a more strenuous nature for about one and a half hours, not only got covered in a substantial layer of Lancashire mud, but then had to queue up for the privilege of washing the mud off their bodies with cold water. Another compulsory organised activity was Padre's hour. This was a weekly informal gathering of one hours duration with the Padre. There were three Padres at Weeton to minister to C of E, Catholics and OD. I'm by birth C of E, but at Weeton I always claimed (with many others) to be OD. I had valid reasons for this deception. As I have written previously it was a very cold and miserable winter. Not only was the OD Padre a gentleman of the first order. He served a good cup of tea, a first class slice of cake and his hut was always warm. On one occasion a high ranking officer from the spiritual branch of the service paid a visit during Padre's hour. I must admit I can not recall the rank of this visiting officer but he was high enough in the pecking order to have scrambled egg on the peak of his cap. This officer asked one of our number why the OD Padre had more men at his meeting than either of the other two Padres did. The airman came back with the immediate answer 'because he has the biggest ruddy fire – sir'. This airman spoke for every man present. In an endeavour to maintain a degree of fitness, it was compulsory for trainees to attend PE sessions. The sessions were under the control of 'old sweat' instructors. Their main objective seemed calculated to avoiding forms of exercise that would cause them any physical grief prior to their retirement from the service. They were certainly more casual and civilised in their approach than the keen young instructors at Bridgnorth. The NAAFI was a popular evening gathering place. It was warm, comfortable but most importantly inexpensive. I never thought much of the tea that was served but the facilities on offer allowed my companions and I time to enjoy many games of billiards and snooker.

As my course progressed, more of my evenings had to be spent in study. It was important for me to do well in my trade test, not only would success lead to interesting work, it would also mean financial reward. The latter was a good incentive to try hard.

I never went to Blackpool in the evenings, not only did it seem a waste of time, it could also be expensive. On occasions I took a walk round the lanes in the vicinity of the camp. During these evening jaunts I often used to drop into a pub in one of the local villages. I used one particular pub quite often. As well as sampling the local brew I often had a game of darts with the local farmers. I was on good terms with many of these farmers and just before Christmas 1955 I purchased a chicken from one of them for 10/6, (52 ½p). It was a good sized bird, which had been plucked but was complete with its head and inners. When I got home with the bird Mary informed me that as she would have to cook it, I could have the task of preparing it. Oh to recapture the carefree days of yesteryear.

Travelling Home - Christmas 1955

Having related how I acquired our Christmas dinner, it would seem the obvious place to relate how I got it home. That of course is my real home in Solihull as opposed to my temporary abode, which was courtesy of HM Government. I never thought of my various postings as home. As Christmas came upon us, most of the 'inmates', (for want of a better description) of Weeton camp would go home for seven days. The camp's essential services would be maintained for the Christmas period by a few Scotsmen who would have their leave over the New Year period. This of course was one of the few, very few, sensible arrangements that existed in the RAF at that time. A special train was to run from Kirkham to London to carry personnel from the RAF camps at Weeton to Kirkham. The train would stop at Preston for personnel to change for more northerly destinations. It was then to proceed via Warrington and Crewe to London. Passengers for Midland destinations would need to change at Crewe. The snag with the special train was that it would be very full; it was reserved solely for the use of RAF personnel as far as Preston. As it was a time of year when so many people needed to travel, it was decided that from Preston onwards civilians could board the train subject, of course, to space availability. I set off for home and the first Christmas Mary and I would spend in our own house. When I set out it was clutching a large suitcase in one hand and a plucked chicken (complete with head) in the other. I started the journey by sitting on my case in the corridor, still clutching the ruddy chicken. The part of the corridor in which I staked my claim was adjacent to a first class compartment which contained several passengers I knew would be changing at Preston. It only took a short time to travel from Kirkham to Preston, so within the matter of minutes I was settled in a corner seat in a first class compartment with my case and chicken deposited on the luggage rack. As the journey progressed I suffered a little discomfort as if I had gone along the corridor to have a pee, some beggar would no doubt have pinched my seat. So I crossed my legs and stuck it out to Crewe. Several civilians boarded the train at its various stops. One elderly lady called the guard and objected to service personnel having first class seats while she had to stand. To his credit the guard remained courteous but firm as he pointed out to this lady and several other civilians within hearing distance, that as the train was primarily for service personnel he was unable to intervene, even if he had wished to, which he didn't as his service passengers were giving no cause for complaint. The remainder of the journey was uneventful, it was in fact boring as my main objective was to get home. I changed at Crewe and was met at Birmingham by Mary. I arrived in Birmingham about one hour late, which by British Railway standards was about normal for that time. I had made this particular journey by means of a travel warrant. To the best of my recollection service personnel received an annual allocation of travel warrants, I believe it was four. From my point of view I considered a warrant should only be used when the maximum advantage could be gained from it. Even in those days I was a calculating beggar who looked for a good deal. A user of pure logic.

Food

As I have previously written food at Weeton was good and plentiful. However, all young men eat a lot, particularly when away from home. My colleagues and I were no exception to this general rule, enjoying particularly our evening snack. We of course had to take into account our restricted financial position when deciding as to what gastronomical delight each one of us would enjoy during the evening. One option was to have supper at about 9.00 p.m. in the airmen's mess. The big point in favour of this option was that it didn't cost anything; there were snags; such as:

1. Supper in the mess depended on food being left over from earlier meals of the day.

2. When meals of the day had been of a particularly favoured content, it was unlikely that any food would be left over.
3. Some foods had very little appeal when served cold or in a reheated state. So apart from a fresh brew up, supper in the mess was a hit and miss affair.

There was always the option of purchasing a locally made hot pie from the vendor who had a pitch by the camp gate. I must concede that his pies were first class, but the cost of 1/- each made them an occasional luxury. I solved my personal evening snack problem by taking food back to camp from my weekend home leave. Mary always packed me enough bread pudding to last for two or three evenings. This was supplemented with a small packet of spread cheeses and a box of cracker biscuits. So I got through to the next weekend with the minimum of expenditure on food.

Barracks and Mess Damages

Damages always seemed to lead to bizarre reasoning and behaviour both from airmen and those who issued orders. I'll deal with barrack room damages first. The most common form this damage took was broken lamp shades. The damage was usually as a result of indoor football, cricket or horseplay of a boisterous nature. This was all totally innocent and non malicious, but unfortunately often ended up by causing damage or breakages. The lamp shades used in billets were of a very basic plastic/celluloid type. Similar lamp shades could be purchased from Woolworths or other High Street stores for about 1/6, (7 ½p) each. The obvious thing for the person breaking the shade was to replace the damaged one with a shade taken from a store room or similar obscure area. He could then purchase a new shade for 1/6 on his next trip to the High Street and make good the obscure shortage. The alternative was to purchase a replacement from the RAF station stores for 4/6, - yes 4/6. This price was as a result of the bizarre authoritive reasoning that was used; the method used to attain this some what inflated figure went thus:

1/6 for breaking a lamp shade, (its value).
Plus 1/6 to purchase a lamp shade from the stores.

Plus 1/6 to replace the lamp shade in the stores.

I'm sure you will agree that this reasoning was so extreme that it bordered on insanity. It would be funny if it were not for the fact that it was the reasoning of persons whose decisions influenced the daily lives of others.

Now for mess damages. It was inevitable that there would be crockery breakages. Drinking mugs didn't count as each person was responsible for their own. Plates got broken by normal use and misuse. Periodically it was announced that each airman would be levied the sum of 1/- towards the cost of replacing broken crockery, the levy to be stopped from each man's pay. This seemed unjust to those who had not broken anything as they still had to pay with no option to refuse. The announcement was always greeted with a noisy response. Unfortunately a few persons of low intelligence often took more drastic action, which in my opinion was totally out of order. What was done by this fringe lunatic element, (such elements exist throughout society) was to fix the leg of a table, so that as a person got up to leave, the table would collapse, spilling and breaking a considerable amount of crockery. The person/s who caused this mishap reasoned in some bizarre way that they had now got value for the levy they had been charged. Strange people.

Clothes and Credits

This aspect of my tale is not exclusive to RAF Weeton, it applied throughout my service career. I have chosen to deal with the subject at this point as it was at Weeton that I attended my first clothing parade. Like all other airmen I received a weekly clothing allowance; on paper. It was permitted for airmen to attend a clothing parade to select their requirements from the stores. Items would be charged for quarterly from the persons credits. At the end of the quarter airmen who were in credit would receive the credit value in their wages. Anybody who had overspent their clothing credits would have the difference stopped from their pay. My personal system was to purchase what was necessary for personal comfort and smartness, whilst just staying in credit. I was fortunate that I 'inherited' a good quality best blue uniform from my father. It was a little used 1940s issue, but was identical in pattern to the 1955 issue. Being in possession of this 'gash' uniform was to save me a considerable amount of clothing credit. I come now to the purpose of my first clothing parade. Airmen who had finished training were permitted to purchase a set of anodised buttons. These of course remained bright without having to be polished on a daily basis with Brasso. So, immediately my training was completed, I presented myself on the first available clothing parade for my set of anodised buttons. It didn't end there as in the true tradition of the service, I then had to sew the ruddy things on.

Chapter 15

DEPARTING PROCEDURE

This was done in true established and long standing service tradition by means of a chit. No doubt the ritual I describe is now achieved in our present highly technical age of computers by the touch of a button. I am however sure that the 1956 method will make more entertaining reading. The departure chit was obtained from station HQ. The basic information on it gave personal details of the airman concerned, date of his ordered departure, reason for his posting and his new location. When the chit was handed to the departing airman, it was then necessary for him to present himself and his chit at every section of the establishment. The objective of the exercise was to communicate the details of the airman's imminent departure to all who needed to know for administration purposes. There was also an arrival chit. It was an established fact that a departing airman could go through this procedure in a couple of hours. However, the same airman with calculated time wasting could take a couple of days to process an arrival chit. Particularly competent skivers have been known to take three days or more to 'arrive', these were the true exponents of the skiver's art.

Throughout my service career I counted the days to when I would have in my hot little hand a departure chitty that would give my reason for departure as 'completion of whole time National Service'. Roll on demob.

Chapter 16

GOODBYE WEETON

At last, my posting order came through. I was given a departure chitty, instructed to have an early breakfast next morning and parade with all my kit at 6.30 a.m. ready for departure. I whistled round with my departure chitty in about two hours on Thursday afternoon. I did well in the time and had full clearance with the exception of one section, sods law always seemed to apply when things were going too well. The exception was the bedding stores. The moronic Corporal in charge flatly refused to sign until I physically handed in my bedding. He had little faith in his fellow beings, particularly airmen, and believed they had an urge to abscond with their hairy blankets, stiff sheets and threadbare pillow cases. So my bedding would have to be handed in before 6.30 a.m. on the following morning, never mind. Justice would be served as the moronic Corporal would have to also get up early to sign for his beloved blankets.

Friday morning came and I was up at 5.30 a.m., I was certainly not up with the lark as it was the middle of winter, dark, cold and the lark had got more sense than to get up at that time in those conditions. I dressed in one minute flat, to have taken longer would have exposed delicate parts of my anatomy to possible frostbite, not a pleasant prospect. Then came a quick dash to the mess for breakfast, my last meal at Weeton. As I left the mess I was handed a bag that contained my rations for the day. These consisted of a 'plastic' egg between two slices of bread. A plastic egg was one that had been fried in deep fat for so long that it was totally encased in a heard plastic like cocoon that made it inedible. The bag also contained a hard, (very hard) boiled egg and a bar of chocolate. I believe the rations were issued to save some faceless airman in admin having to get up early to hand out subsistence allowance.

It was then back to the billet for the last time, for the purpose of packing the last few items of my kit and of course collect my bedding for return to the stores. I left it as long as possible before I took my bedding to stores, this gave me the satisfaction of keeping a certain storekeeper from his breakfast. When I finally got the last signature on my departure chitty I presented it at station HQ where it was changed for a travel warrant to cover my rail journey to Abingdon on Thames, third class of course. My three colleagues and I duly paraded at 6.30 a.m. with our full kit to await the transport for the first stage of what would prove to be an epic day of travel. It was as well that each of the four of us was blessed with a good level of intelligence. Nobody had issued any specific instructions as to how our transfer was to be achieved as several changes of train would be necessary. It could well happen that airmen of low intelligence may well travel in the completely wrong direction in these circumstances. We fortunately did not have this problem. It was cold, it was so cold that whilst I stood there in front of Weeton HQ, it would have come as no surprise if I had seen a screaming brass monkey run past looking for a welder. The transport arrived; not a coach; not a car; but an ancient open top Bedford wagon. Thank goodness it was only a couple of miles to the railway station. So shortly after 6.30 a.m. our reluctant quartet, complete with kit, packed lunches and apprehension, departed from No. Eight S of T T, (Royal Air Force, Weeton, Lancashire) for the last time.

The rail journey was less than two hundred miles, but my companions and I had studied the map and calculated that we would have to change trains in the region of five times. The first part of the journey to Birmingham, (New Street) was uneventful, if one ignores having to change at Preston and Crewe. Birmingham was the first major test of stamina as it was necessary to change stations. Being a Brummie I knew the route to take, nevertheless the task was physically tough as the centre of Birmingham was not the flattest of city centres. We eventually boarded a train for Oxford. Under a different set of circumstances, to travel from Snowhill, through the tunnel in a southerly direction; on a train which was hauled by a king class Great Western locomotive would have been a pleasure. On this occasion it was certainly not a pleasure. It was in fact frustrating in the extreme. Shortly after leaving Birmingham the train went through Olton station which was within a mile of my home. To make it even more frustrating it was at about the time that Mary would have been arriving home from work. That stage of the journey continued without incident and we arrived at Oxford. Time had moved on, it was now early evening with a chill in the air. There was still the prospect of two more trains to catch. Abingdon on Thames is only a few miles from Oxford, but that winter evening in 1956 British Railways made it seem as if it was the far side of the world. Considering the total lack of instructions as to the complexities of our journey, we'd done alright, up to now. We eventually boarded a local train which would get us a few miles further to Radley, the station at which we would make the last change. The train that had brought us to Radley departed and we stood on the platform and waited. I must admit that my companions and I were totally unprepared for what happened next. It was as if we had suddenly entered a time warp, out of the darkness heading towards us was a very ancient GWR Celestry coach that by rights should have been pensioned off to a museum years earlier. That was not all, as the coach got to the platform I saw that it was being pushed by an even more ancient GWR shunting engine. I was lucky being able to see any of this due to the amount of steam that was leaking from the locomotive. This apparition was our final train of the day. It was known as 'The Abingdon Flyer' and provided a shuttle service between Radley and the dead end station at Abingdon, which was at the end of a one station spur line. Our knackered quartet were the only passengers for the trip, so once aboard we set off with much leaking of steam and triumphant whistling from the loco. We got to Abingdon without mishap and made our way to a deserted station forecourt. It was even colder, thank goodness I'd had a pee at Oxford. It was now about 9.00 p.m. and of course there was no waiting transport. The Station Master was good enough to phone the aerodrome and advise them of our arrival. After what seemed hours, but what in fact was no more than fifteen minutes, transport arrived. Typical RAF transport in the shape of a small Austin pick up truck which did at least have the refinement of a canvas tilt. The four of us, complete with kit squeezed into the back with the sundry tat that was already there. It was only about a mile to the RAF Station at Abingdon so within a few minutes the driver deposited us in front of the guardroom. Hoorah – journey's end. The Orderly Sergeant emerged, asked a few questions. He instructed us to deposit our kit in the guardroom. He then conducted us to the airmen's mess and instructed the Duty Cook to serve us a meal. He left us to enjoy our meal having instructed us to report to the Orderly Officer at the guardroom in half an hour. The meal was consumed and enjoyed. It was then time to report to the Orderly Officer. He greeted us in a courteous manner and said we were in fact not expected until Monday. He explained that Abingdon was holding one of its very rare parades on Saturday as a result of which the station HQ would be closed. He suggested that if we would like to 'get lost' until Monday he was prepared to issue the necessary passes to make our absence official. This man was truly an officer and a gentleman. As all four of us lived in the southern part of the country his offer was accepted with enthusiasm.

So armed with my leave pass and my kit safely deposited in the guardroom cell, it was goodbye to RAF Abingdon for a couple of days at least. I set off to learn a new hitch hiking route home, a free man until I reported to station HQ at 9.00 a.m. on Monday.

Chapter 17

RAF ABINGDON ON THAMES

(THE SECOND COMING)

This was to be my official arrival as opposed to my first brief 'visit' which was late in the evening on the previous Friday. A visit that I would not have made had I been a little more experienced in the art of skiving. I learned quickly.

After my brief, unexpected, enjoyable weekend at home the time came to return to RAF Abingdon. Having no knowledge of any special travel arrangements that may have existed I decided to travel on the Sunday evening by train. After my experience the previous Friday evening I thought it best to avoid using the 'Abingdon Flyer' and travelled from Oxford by bus. This worked out alright and of course gave me the option of hitch hiking if the bus plan misfired. I arrived at the RAF station gates at about 10.00 p.m., I would have liked to have spent a little more time at home, but I had erred on the side of caution as trains were very limited during the winter timetable. Come to think of it, the Summer timetable wasn't much better. On arrival I duly reported to the guardroom and in the company of other newly arrived airmen, snatched a few hours sleep in the corner of a guardroom cell. Monday morning dawned, after a wash and shave it was down to the mess for my first Abingdon breakfast. The meal was good, the only bad point was the sight of the usual compulsory tray of runny 'pom'. I reported to HQ bang on 9.00 a.m., sorry 0900 hours, to commence my official arrival procedure.

The Corporal Clerk expected me and was good enough to take a little time to give me some basic gen that would prove useful in carrying out my arrival formalities. At that time RAF Abingdon was part of transport command. It was the home of the Parachute training school and a balloon unit, the activities of which were associated with the parachute training school. He issued me with my arrival chit and the information that I would be allocated to 1312 flight. He suggested I make the 1312 office my first port of call as I could then be allocated a bed in a billet with other ground crew members of the flight. I found my way to the flights hangar and reported to the Chiefie in charge. This particular Chiefie was an ex aircrew Flight Sergeant Engineer who was well experienced in the ways of the service, thank goodness my new boss was to be a practical man of experience as opposed to some immature academic. After exchanging brief courtesies, the Flight Clerk allocated me a billet, suggested I draw my blankets from the stores and get settled in. Chiefie then said I should carry on with my arrival procedure and report back to him in a couple of days when my arrival was completed. It was obvious that this Chiefie had no desire to bug what was a long and excepted service procedure. I was already beginning to like the guy. After drawing my bedding I made my way to the billet. What a surprise! To this point my service accommodation had been in primitive oversized wooden sheds, with even more primitive detached toilet and washing facilities. What I walked into at Abingdon was a two storey brick built building with first class built in toilets and bathrooms. This was not all, there was no coke burning stove or lino covered floor, but an efficient central heating system and polished wooden floors. I in fact rechecked the room number as I believed I had perhaps wandered into the Sergeants' or Officers' accommodation in error. No, I was in the right place, hooray for the real air force. Without further ado I staked my claim to a spare bed and fetched my kit from the guardroom. It was now lunch time and some of the 1312 ground crew returned to the billet for a wash before proceeding to the mess. Some rapid introductions took place and I accompanied some of my new colleagues to lunch. Over the meal my new friends filled me in on the flight and station set up. The important facts, such as the CO not being a great advocate of unnecessary bull, that was good news. As long as his personnel kept themselves and the station clean and tidy, caused no trouble (particularly when off base) and kept the aircraft well serviced and operational, he was a happy man. To one who had spent most of his time, up to that moment in training establishments, this sounded like Utopia, in fact a thoroughly good show. After lunch I spent the rest of the day 'arriving', this was a particularly useful exercise as it also gave me a good idea of the geographical layout of what was to be my home for over a year. In the evening, over the compulsory glass of ale in the NAAFI, I learned a bit more about the physical operational strength of the station. The main aircraft that were operated by all squadrons and flights were Handley Page Hastings, a product of impeccable pedigree.

In addition 1312 also had three Vickers Valettas, (the military version of the Viking), and was also responsible for the operational serviceability of three De Havilland Chipmunks. So it looked as if I was about to enter an interesting stage of my service at a busy aerodrome. That night in the Abingdon billet was the first night I had been warm during the entire winter of 1955/56. The following morning was spent in the reading and signing of what seemed an endless number of books of standing orders. At that time the RAF had volumes of orders and instructions, coupled with a misguided view that if an airman read an order and signed that he had read it, he had fully understood it and had it forever etched on his memory. What a load of bull. The afternoon was spent with the Chiefie in charge of 1312 mechanics. He first explained my duties and issued me with a tool kit, for which I had to sign. My duties to start with would be the routine service of Bristol and De Havilland engines on the flights aircraft. When I had gained some practical experience I would be promoted to LAC and allocated to a specific aircraft. My hours of work would be from 0800 hours until 1700 hours, with early and late duties as necessary. If however it was necessary to work after 2000 hours I would be permitted to have one hour off the following morning for each hour of late duty performed. This was particularly good if Friday night work carried on up to midnight as it meant having Saturday morning off. This meant an early start home for the weekend. I would also have to attend trade training classes to enable me to take an examination for promotion to SAC. He went on to say that ground crew were encouraged to fly in the aircraft they serviced as it helped to make them more efficient and careful tradesmen. At the end of our talk he dismissed me with orders to report to him at 0800 hours the following morning. As my first couple of days as a ground crew member at RAF Abingdon drew to an end I felt that if I could not be at home with my dear wife, Abingdon had distinct advantages over some of the foreign holes I could have ended up in.

Handley Page Hastings of 1312FLT. Taken by author in 1956 at Castel Beneto (Idris) Libya.

CHAPTER 18

1312 FLIGHT

(ITS MAKEUP AND PURPOSE)

Its full title was 1312 TSF (Transport Support Flight). This title was later changed to TSE (Transport Support Element). Strange, as the function of the flight remained unaltered, no doubt some chairbound wingless wonder in Whitehall conceived the meaningless change, typical. I have previously mentioned the three types of aircraft for which we were responsible. All three models had a slang name. In the case of the Hastings it was known as a 'haystack', the Valetta was called a 'pig', this was possibly due to its ungainly appearance when viewed from the front as it stood on the ground. Finally the little De Havilland Chipmunk was affectionately called a 'chippie'. The flights operational centre was a hangar and dispersal well away from the more civilised areas of the station. This arrangement seemed sensible as at times the tasks of the flight would be a little unusual. Most of the routine flying activities were allied to the needs of the parachute training school. There were other joint operations involving the army and their training programme for the provision of supplies dropped by air. The Hastings was such a versatile aircraft that it could rapidly be converted to different roles. The range of roles was huge, such as carrying of passengers in conventional aircraft seats, paratroop role with provision to drop troops simultaneously from both sides of the plane. In its various guises for carrying freight it could be 'gutted' so that the fuselage could be totally devoted to freight carrying. Alternatively roller conveyors could be fitted to allow heavy supplies to be rapidly discharged for dropping by parachute. Externally bomb racks could be fitted under the wings for the dropping of supply canisters. Without a doubt the most impressive was to see a military jeep dropped by parachute from where it was suspended under the fuselage. So life was never dull on 1312.

At times the flight would have to provide aircraft for route flying. This meant conveying people or supplies to or from any location world wide. In the case of the Hastings an engine and airframe mechanic often travelled on the aircraft. Route flights were always popular with ground crew as it gave a chance to travel without actually being posted overseas. During my time with 1312 I went to places such as Malta, Iraq, Libya and many others, more of that later. The Chipmunks the flight maintained were very popular with the pilots of all squadrons. This was particularly so in the case of some of the younger pilots who seemed to look upon doing aerobatics in the chippie as a way of letting off a bit of steam. I always kept a seat parachute in my locker and never missed the chance to fly in a chippie when I had the time and the pilot was prepared to take me. I admit that I found the exhilaration of this type of flying particularly enjoyable, particularly such things as loops and stall turns. The seat in the chippie was of pressed metal construction with a recess that housed the parachute which served as a cushion. When kitted out in a seat parachute, the wearer had a most peculiar walk which gave the appearance that he was either suffering from an unsocial disease or diarrhoea. This was not so, however the second complaint may well have affected faint hearted airmen after they experienced aerobatics for the first time.

Chapter 19

1312 FLIGHT - PEOPLE

When I arrived at the real air force, by that I mean the operational side of the service as opposed to the training side, the first observation was that I had moved from a dictatorship to a democracy. 1312 flight was a classical example, particularly on the air crew side. A typical crew may well consist of a mixture of commissioned and non commissioned officers of varying ranks, this caused no problems and on occasions a Flight Sergeant or Master Pilot may well have been the aircraft's Captain. The flights air crew members ranged from Sergeant to Squadron Leader. Ground staff were from AC2 to Warrant Officer, with several airmen of various ranks and technical ability in each trade that was necessary to keep the planes in first class readiness and repair. In the case of engine and airframe mechs., it was the practice to be number one mechanic on a specific aircraft and to assist as number two on another. The arrangement was reciprocal, as the mechanic I assisted was in turn my number two. This arrangement had the advantage of maintaining continuity if one of a pair went on leave or had duties away from his normal work place. I was number one on Hastings WD498 and assistant on WD495. In addition to our own aircraft it was necessary to muck in on the servicing of the Valettas and Chipmunks. In the case of the ground tradesmen we were roughly a fifty fifty mix of National Service and career personnel. Both types worked well together and no obvious friction occurred.

"Blackburn Beverley"

Chapter 20

CHARACTERS

They belong to a breed of persons that are vastly different to the rest of mankind. They have individual characteristics such as dress, physical features, behaviour patterns or other personal attributes that set them apart from their fellow beings. Characters should not be confused with types who set out to be different by following trends, these people are totally transparent and boring. At the higher levels of the social pecking order appearance of genuine characters rarely offends, as their style is not a designer form of individuality as in the case of types. The things that make people characters are often so innocent as to border on simplicity. During my long and varied working life I have been privileged to have known and associated with many characters. I found my time in the RAF a wonderful and rare opportunity to carry out some serious character observations in depth. Living and working so closely with people of an assorted range of social backgrounds over a prolonged period made character observing an enjoyable and inexpensive pastime. I now take the opportunity to write on some of the characters I knew at Royal Air Force Abingdon. I purposely mention no names, (I do however remember each one, even their nicknames). If my book goes into print and is read by any of my 'characters', I shall be most flattered if they recognise themselves from my written descriptions of them.

The popular music of the time was 'skiffle' of which the principal exponent was Lonnie Donegan. This particular form of musical art was totally unsophisticated, yet was lively, melodious in its own way, and was enjoyable to listen to. The trendy male dress of the time was drain pipe trousers, preferably black. These facts are essential background and introduction to my first character. The young man in question was well educated, musically gifted, trendy in his dress but totally individual. In fact a truly text book character. His off duty dress was black (very black) drain pipe trousers and black tee shirt. This was fine, except he slept in these clothes and when he got up each morning he put his uniform on over this outfit.

At the end of the working day he would remove his uniform, to reveal his well worn and creased socialising outfit. Ugh. I must admit to having no personal knowledge of him ever removing his trendy clothes during the time I was billeted with him, a period in excess of one year. I have already mentioned he was a gifted musician who was able to give a reasonable rendering on the guitar and cornet. He was a cornet player in the station band. Unfortunately he tended to practice in the billet at unsocial hours. The ultimate for this character was when he got back to the billet on Sunday night after his weekend at home. He would alight from the coach that brought him from London, make the short walk from the camp gates to the billet. He was of course dressed in his usual black, creased drain pipes and tee shirt. His next move was to deposit himself in a sitting position on his bed, unfortunately the next one to mine. When settled comfortably he would remove his shoes and socks and give his toes their weekly pick. Toes that on most occasions I saw them were allied in colour to his trousers.

This character was an engine mechanic, but was employed on the refuelling section. This work kept him away from other persons for most of his working day. I never did discover if he did this particular job out of choice because he was a loner, or if it had been calculated by some higher authority as a back handed way of segregating him; makes you think. It could well have been contrived because of his peculiar behaviour pattern.

My next character was an artistic type, who always carried his sketch book and pencil. Presumably in the hope that he may see some event or sight that would be worthy of a quick sketch. Like my first character, he was also musical. He played the guitar and cornet, after a fashion, but acceptably, thank goodness. On one occasion he was on a route flight to a base in the South of France. As a matter of routine his sketch book went with him. His sketches on this occasion were destined to be different, very different to his normal type of work. The hostelry he chose to use for his evening drink doubled as the local establishment of ill repute. When he sat at his table and produced his sketch book and proceeded to make a few drawings of the scene, he was observed with interest by some of the ladies who worked in the establishment. These ladies not only admired his work, but wished to be part of it. The result was that some of them sat facing him across the table in various poses and states of undress. When he returned to the UK his colleagues without exception, voted the work he had done in France as his best to date.

I bet some of my readers are persons who are unable to 'come too' in the mornings without a cup of tea or coffee. My next character was such a person, he needed 'a fix' before he could get his head from under the blankets. Not for him tea or coffee, his particular poison was a Woodbine and a ruddy good cough. No way could he leave the land of nod without his fix. His last job at night was to place a box of matches on the top of his bedside locker with one Woodbine sticking out of the box at a rampant angle. It was also important that the box be placed in a precise position on the locker. When he awoke in the morning his hand would emerge from within the bed, (whilst his head remained under the covers) home in on the Woodbine and matches, drawing them into his bed, almost too quickly for the human eye to see. On occasions people would move the cigarette to a different spot on his locker. The result was to see his hand groping around in sheer panic when it failed to home in immediately on its goal.

My final Abingdon character was a character with a capital 'C'. I have purposely left him to last, as I personally consider him to be the perfect text book character. His total innocence and general easy going demeanor was instrumental in putting him at the forefront in the character stakes.

He was a reserved and physically 'plump' young man with a studious nature. Not for him hard physical sport, dirty jokes or boozing with the boys. He got a great deal of personal pleasure and satisfaction from reading and studying. His favourite subject was theology and he spent a considerable amount of time at the local library reading as much as he could on the subject. He had an ambition to eventually join the Church and become a Clergyman. I don't know if he achieved his ambition, I hope he did as he was such a nice guy. However, I doubt that he did attain his goal on account of his personal problem. He suffered with flatulence. In fact to be perfectly frank and totally truthful, it was a problem of monumental proportions. Not for him the genteel carpet slippered and almost silent hiss of escaping air; but hearty shirt shifting throaty farts that could be heard at a hundred paces, or more. They were more suited to a connoisseur of the art of breaking wind than a would be man of the cloth.

I suggest he could well be a candidate for a form of minor surgery that I believe has now been perfected, (if it hasn't it should be). The surgery I have in mind is a 'fartectomy'; as with a vasectomy it is carried out under local anaesthetic. It basically consists of a quick snip in the right place. In this case the right place is the farting clapper. The characters of Abingdon were many and varied. The four I have written about were but a few that I was privileged to have known. They are however the ones I believe to be the best examples of what constitutes a character.

Chapter 21

EXTENDED TRAINING

Training was an ongoing thing in the RAF, especially in the case of tradesmen. Soon after starting work as a member of 1312 ground crew I was promoted to LAC. Extended training now became more important to me, not only would it equip me for more interesting work, but would take me to the stage of being able to take my trade test for promotion to SAC. I reached this stage within a couple of months of joining 1312, largely as a result of practical experience gained during that period. The trade test came round and I was delighted to pass at first attempt. I was immediately promoted to SAC, not only did this put me on a par with most of my colleagues, it removed me from the slot of new boy, but most importantly gave me a few extra bob in my pocket. For the remainder of my service at Abingdon it was a requirement that I attend a short monthly training session on service and current affairs. I admit to enjoying these one hour sessions, not only from their interesting content but also from the resulting stimulating discussions that were generated.

Shortly after my promotion to SAC I was offered a place on a one week's specialist training course at a civilian establishment. There was no hesitation in accepting what had been offered. The course was on variable pitch propellers and was to be held at the De Havilland propeller factory at Walkden in Lancashire. The factory was in an old converted textile mill on the outskirts of Manchester. Two other members of 1312 would be with me. My companions would be another SAC and an old sweat Chief Technician Engine Fitter. The SAC was younger than me and a little immature, but he had an eye for the girls, even if his line of chat was a bit corny. The Chiefie was within a couple of years of retirement, a bit of a philosopher, in fact an excellent and amiable companion, in spite of the difference in age and rank. The course was scheduled to start on a Monday morning and accommodation had been reserved from Sunday night for the 1312 trio. I was handed a rail warrant to travel to Manchester via Birmingham and Crewe, this of course was a bonus to me as it would mean a weekend at home with no personal travelling expenses. It meant two weekends as the operation could be reversed at the conclusion of the course.

With the warrant was a chitty which informed me that a room had been reserved for me at the King George Services Hotel in Piccadilly, Manchester. This sounded rather grand for a mere SAC, never mind, I'd been in the RAF long enough to be philosophical and accept orders without question.

After a pleasant weekend at home, Sunday evening came and with it the need to travel to Manchester. There being no direct convenient train from Birmingham to Manchester it would be necessary to change at Crewe, in the middle of the night. I eventually got to Manchester shortly after midnight. I emerged from the station to go and search for my hotel. I quickly spotted a huge, ancient, ugly building which bore on it a sign that informed everybody that it was the King George Services Hotel. It also bore a second sign that had the letters YMCA on it, oh what a let down. My accommodation was not quite as grand as I had imagined it would be. The let down was not yet complete as the single room accommodation was little more than a hardboard cubicle, similar to several dozen more which were located in a huge dusty barn like room that smelt of dust, sweaty bodies and stale farts. The disillusionment was completed by the furnishing of the garret which consisted of an iron framed single bed and a clothes locker, the latter of which had a door that had to be secured by means of a padlock.

I met up with my colleagues from Abingdon at Monday breakfast. It was obvious from the conversation over the meal that they were no more impressed with the accommodation than I was. The meal was a basic, very basic, self service affair which had to be paid for before consumption, the cost of this gastronomical nightmare was 2/6 (12 ½p). After breakfast the three of us set off by bus to travel to the De Havilland factory at Walkden, arriving there in good time, inspite of it being the Manchester morning rush hour. After a brief introduction to our instructors and other members of the course, it was to work. The course was enjoyable and consisted of lectures combined with practical demonstrations and exercises in the factory. The latter part of this came easily to me as most of my civilian working life had been in a large factory. The other thing that commended the course was the fact that we had a substantial and free midday meal in the works canteen. This was very much appreciated due to the basic dining facilities at our accommodation and the low level of subsistence allowance from the RAF. Although the members of the course were a delightful crowd, the three of us from Abingdon stuck together for our social activities. My fellow SAC and I always wore our civilian clothes in the evenings, but Chiefie who was the third member of the trio wore his best gabardine uniform, complete with ribbons. It was his contention that his inverted stripes (the American style) was a good opening for conversation. During the week at Manchester we visited the ballroom at the Bell Vue complex and experienced some north country entertainment at Tommy's Music Hall. The latter was in what to the best of my recollection was the Devonshire Hotel, which contained the biggest bar that I have ever been in, and I've been in a few.

The course finished at lunch time on Friday. However, I clearly remember staying at the factory long enough to have a meal. It was then a short final trip back to the City by bus, for the purpose of collecting our kit prior to bidding goodbye to that northern city. The three of us set out on the short walk to the station and were surprised by the number of 'ladies of the town' we saw, they seemed to be standing in every shop doorway we passed during our short walk. I presume this was as it was Friday which was traditionally the pay day of industrial and office workers. Our little trio departed from Manchester on the same train. I bid my companions farewell at Crewe as I was going to get a train home for the weekend. My companions remained on the original train, 'Smudge', my fellow SAC, to his home in London and Chiefie back home to his married quarters at RAF Abingdon. The course had been good, the company had been good, the change of daily routine had been good and to top it off I was having a long weekend at home, a good show all round.

After my weekend at home, it was back to RAF Abingdon. Work

was never dull on 1312, largely due to the flight being well blessed with 'characters'. In spite of this it was still a welcome break to be employed away from the normal routine. This was why a training course away from base was always attractive and welcome. More especially if it was conducted at a civilian establishment, with the added attraction of civilian accommodation. I was destined to attend one more civilian course during my service career. It was to be of two weeks duration and based on the Bristol Hercules sleeve valve engine. This particular course was to be held in the aero engine training complex at the Filton factory of the Bristol Aircraft Company, a place that I had passed on many occasions during family holiday trips to the west country, pre motorway of course. Accommodation was to be in a lodging house in the outer suburbs of Bristol and about one mile from the factory. The course was during late 1956, it had to be late in the year as it was so cold. At least on this occasion I would be spared the ordeal of sleeping in a wooden hut as I had during the previous winter's training in Lancashire. Earlier in that year I had obtained a small modest car. It was a two seater, soft top 1932 Austin Seven with wire wheels. An ideal fun car for a young airman and his pretty wife. The £25 it cost me seemed rather a lot, but it was well worth it for the amount of pleasure it gave us. Having the car allowed me to draw travelling expenses for a double return trip from Abingdon to Bristol, in addition to this I drew two weeks wages, meal allowance and the lodging fees for my civilian landlady. It was about this time that petrol rationing was introduced as a direct result of the Middle East conflict which had closed the Suez canal. This reminds me that when the canal closed the oil companies put a surcharge of 1/- on a gallon of petrol to offset the extra cost of having to route tankers round the Cape instead of through the Suez Canal. Come to think of it, I have no recollection of the companies ever taking the surcharge off, robbing beggars.

Another national event of that time was the announcement of a premium bond scheme. With single units of £1 each, being on sale at Post Offices. On the weekend prior to the course I managed to get home, but due to the petrol situation I decided I would leave my car at home and travel to Bristol by train on Sunday evening. When I arrived at Bristol it was necessary to get a bus from the City to Filton. I had fortunately been given some details of local landmarks, (pubs) close to my digs so I had little trouble in alighting from the bus at the correct landmark. A quick enquiry in the pub and I was off walking in the correct direction. I eventually reached the large typical suburban semi which was to be my temporary home for the duration of my two weeks at Bristol aircraft. I was greeted at the door by the lady who ran these premises. She was without doubt a text book example of the battle-axe type of landlady who was the butt of numerous comedians' jokes. She ushered me into the guests' lounge cum dining room, even its comfortable furnishings and warmth couldn't disguise the fact that it was a converted garage. There were six of us lodged at these digs, two per bedroom, but we fortunately had our own beds. All six of us would be attending the same course. Each of us came from a different unit and ranged in rank from the LAC to an aircrew Flight Sergeant. We were a good old fashioned mixed bag.

One of my fellow lodgers made a lasting impression on my memory. This was no doubt as a result of the open (but amusing) hostility that existed between him and our landlady. I have to concede that she was a funny beggar who had a very short fuse. At the time of our occupation of this lady's house, eggs were in short supply, but this lady obviously knew somebody as she had a plentiful supply of them. This was obvious as she served them at an above average frequency for the time. The particular lodger I write about used to annoy her by perching on the rail which surrounded the upstairs landing each morning and give his impression of a chicken. He also used to drop out a considerable amount of strong language. On the occasions the landlady walked in whilst he was cussing, he would look her straight in the face and say, 'Sorry lady I thought you'd pissed off'.

As the factory was only about a mile from the digs and most of our time at the factory would be spent sitting down it was mutually agreed that it would be sensible to walk to and from the factory. Apart from the exercise it would save the bus fare. I admit that some of the bus fare I saved was spent on sampling the local brew, I was not impressed as it seemed rather colourless and tasteless, in many ways similar to the 4x kangaroo piss that the Australians now pass off as beer.

Of the course itself there were about twelve of us on it, with our principal instructor being an ex Fleet Air Arm Chief Petty Officer

Engineer. As he went through the different aspects of the Hercules engine he had a habit of saying 'that's favourite'. We quickly realised this was his way of indicating the type of questions that would be contained in the trade proficiency examination at the conclusion of the course. There seems little point in describing the technicalities of the course, other than to say that it was instructive and enjoyable. More so as it was conducted in the type of factory environment in which I had spent my civilian working career.

In spite of the landlady being a bit of a tyrant she kept our quarters clean but more importantly fed us well. On one occasion when she was in a talkative mood she spoke of a Warrant Officer who had stayed at her house a couple of years earlier. She related that he spent most of his evenings with some local unsavoury characters in the pub, he then returned to the digs, sat on the front wall with his drunken companions and sang loudly into the night, to the annoyance of the local residents. She thought him a dreadful person and definitely not a gentleman. I must concede to having the same feelings about him. There was little doubt that the landlady had described in minute detail the Warrant Officer of my flight. I later mentioned to him that I believed I had stayed at the digs he had used in Bristol. His reaction was to say something unpleasant about the landlady. I must admit that I had behaved like the perfect diplomat when this lady had related her tale of woe. In the best traditions of cowardice I kept my mouth shut and said nowt, on reflection I was perhaps too frightened to tell her I knew the man.

Like all good things the engine course came to an end and with it my formal specialist trade training. At a much later date, closer to the end of my service engagement, several of my colleagues went on a fire fighting course at Moreton in Marsh. The reason given was that they would on release go onto the reserve as auxiliary firemen. I believe the real reason was that the RAF had a surplus of personnel in some trades and needed to find something for these bods to do. I did not feel cheated by not being selected for one of these courses. I certainly had no desire to be chased up and down a ladder by some civilian fireman. Another important factor was that the timing of this particular course would have adversely affected by freetime at home. As I was in my last few weeks of service and my wife was expecting our first child, my time at home was sacred.
AUTHOR'S NOTE

During the time I was writing this chapter in long hand, I also wrote to the Commanding Officer of RAF Abingdon with a request. I have a book which is entitled 'The first fifty years' and is a brief illustrated history of RAF Abingdon. I believed the CO would be the custodian of the book's copyright, so it was to him I wrote requesting permission to use some of the excellent aircraft photographs it contained. On the day I completed the typing of this chapter I received a reply to my letter. This reply was totally unexpected as it was from Dalton Barracks, Abingdon informing me that the RAF had vacated the barracks (not even the courtesy to refer to it as the airfield) to the army. It would seem that a combination of Politicians, Whitehall Warriors, Civil Servants and sundry parasites in general had achieved something that our enemies couldn't. As I write this many thoughts are running through my mind some happy, some sad, some of annoyance with our system, but mainly that I must write at least one of them down as an epitaph to RAF Abingdon on Thames.

This experience is dedicated to the men and aircraft of RAF Abingdon of yesteryear and is intended my epitaph to them.

On many occasions as I drove back to the drome along the Cumnor to Abingdon road, an aircraft would simultaneously be silently gliding in on its final approach over Boars Hill. As I quietly drove on with my thoughts, the aircraft would get closer and often as it glided a few feet over my head the pilot would give the engines a final burst of throttle to ensure a good landing. I would be startled by the sudden noise, but not too startled to utter the words 'stupid beggar' or similar oath.

No more will motorists be startled in this way on quiet evenings. Or will they? Who knows? Maybe a ghostly aircraft of yesteryear flown by its ghostly crew may still approach over Boars Hill to haunt those who caused the demise of that ghostly crews aerodrome.

In the Austin 7 I owned when at RAF Abingdon 1956.

Chapter 22

ABINGDON ANECDOTES AND HAPPENINGS

Any person who has been a member of the armed services will know, there was and probably still is a system that required military personnel to sign for practically everything they received or did. This first anecdote is about some nameless airman's spontaneous remark regarding this signing syndrome. In the flights hangar was a small office that was the sacred retreat of Chiefie, a hallowed hole that was barred to all unless summoned to enter. The office had an ante room in which ground crew tended to congregate when they had nothing better to do. On one occasion a member of the gathering in this annexe broke wind, there was no doubt what the noise was. It was long, lingering, loud and was accompanied by a most foul smell. It was so vile that Chiefie was prompted to shout from his inner sanctum 'whose shit?', to which somebody shouted back 'yours if you like, sign on the dotted line'. Needless to say when a very red faced Chiefie burst out of his office, the annexe was empty.

I remember a certain Group Captain who when he entertained Officers from other branches of the services liked to take them for a flight in a chippie. He seemed to derive great pleasure from these flights after giving a guest a large lunch in the mess. His pleasure also appeared to be heightened if the guest was of a nervous disposition. What a sadistic CO, but I liked him. On one particular occasion he entertained a naval officer. After a good lunch, Groupie brought his hapless guest to the flights dispersal and ordered that he be fitted with a seat parachute. When this was done Groupie told his passenger what the procedure would be in the case of an emergency. I must admit that my colleagues and I had heard this spiel on many occasions, but still listened in awe as Groupie, with his fine use of the English language systematically reduced his guest to a nervous wreck. Part of his spiel was to explain that the escape panel in the cockpit canopy was too small to allow a portly naval officer to get through when he was wearing a parachute, also if it were necessary to use the parachute it was essential to hold onto the operating pull as it carried a 2/6 deposit. He then took off on the perimeter track, gave a fine display of low level aerobatics, made a fine three point landing. He taxied in with the cockpit canopy open, a satisfied grin on his face and a very air sick passenger. Not the slightest doubt in my mind that Groupie was a character of the first order. These escapades of Groupies were only marred by the fact that some poor soul of an airframe fitter had to clean out the cockpit, thank God I was an engine wallah.

The station cinema was always popular as it had reasonably up to date films and admission charges far lower than civilian cinemas. In spite of security procedures there was a person who on many occasions got a bicycle bulb horn into the building. Uproar would ensue on occasions as the hero kissed the heroin, a sudden 'beep-beep' would be heard as our phantom anonymous horn blower played his trump card.

I can honestly say with hand on heart, I never knew who the phantom beeper was.

On occasions an airman would desire to skive off early from his day's work. There could be various reasons for this, the most common being that the airman involved had an important date in a town or village which was a considerable distance from base. When the colleagues of any man who was attempting to skive off spotted him, there was a well used and proven tactic used to frustrate his best efforts. He was permitted to almost get to the hangar door, completely ignored by the rest of the personnel, who carried on with their normal tasks. However, as the would be skiver was about to step over the threshold to freedom, a chant suddenly went up from all the personnel in the hangar. It went thus, 'there he goes on his toes, skiving off I suppose, wonder if the Chiefie knows?'. It only took seconds for Chiefie to be on the scene, but never quick enough to catch the would be skiver, who by that time was hard at work at his normal tasks.

Later in my service career numbers 24 and 47 squadrons converted to the giant Blackburn Beverley transport aircraft. I once saw a strange sight involving a Beverley. The aircraft built up to take off speed on the runway, the nose lifted but the nose wheels parted company with the aircraft and careered on down the runway to eventually disappear through the hedge which surrounded the drome.

At the end of the runway was a chequered van which housed an odd assortment of bods, who had an equally odd assortment of jobs. One of these bods was the tyre checker. Although aircraft wheels had a tightly controlled limit on the number of landings and take offs they could do, it was customary for an airframe mechanic to carry out a brief visual inspection of tyres before an aircraft took off. To check the tail wheel on the Hastings it was necessary for the checker to lie on the ground and crawl under the rear of the fuselage. Not a pleasant task at any time, it could be even more unpleasant for new inexperienced checkers who did not understand the aircrew's sense of humour. Directly above the tail wheel was the outlet pipe from the aircraft urinal. When the new unsuspecting tyre checker was well and truly stuck under the fuselage, a member of the crew would have a pee with the result that the poor hapless tyre checker got christened, by being peed on from a great height.

One of the groupies I served under walked with a stoop, which I believe was as a result of a war time injury. Additional to this the station mascot was a goat. Not just a goat, but a great mean beggar of a goat. Whenever there was a station parade the goat walked behind Groupie. The station personnel used to lay odds on how long it would be before the goat butted Groupie's rear end. Unfortunately for those of us who had indulged in a little wager, he never did. I recall with considerable trepidation an occasion when we had to parade in Abingdon. As the station held the freedom of the town, it was necessary for us to enter the town on formal occasions with fixed bayonets. As the distance to town was in the region of a mile it would be necessary to carry out the shoulder change drill movement several times. This was a difficult movement when standing still. It was more difficult on the move and particularly so as many of the station personnel had not done any formal drill training for many years. I'm still haunted by the sight of the bayonet that was bobbing about before my eyes as it was fixed to a rifle which was being shouldered by a short, elderly chief technician who was bad on his feet and in an advanced state of knackerisation by the time we reached town. For the return to camp I made sure I was behind a tall airman.

Periodically my turn came round to do a week as a member of the duty crew. The specific task of the duty crew was to attend to visiting aircraft. This involved marshalling the aircraft on its arrival, refuelling, any service that may be required and finally starting it up and seeing it away at the end of its stay. This was of course in addition to one's normal day to day duties. During one of my stints on duty crew the AOC in C made his annual inspection. As a crew member I was excused the parade as I would be caring for his aircraft. The programme was that when his aircraft arrived, it was to be marshalled to the rear of a hangar which was a considerable distance from the parade area. The plan was for him to disembark from his aircraft and transfer to a limousine for the short trip to the parade ground. What a load of bull and monumental waste of resources. His plane arrived, he emerged, not the tall upright dashing officer that I expected, but a short portly man. It was then obvious that the car was necessary to enable him to arrive at the parade with a degree of dignity. He was followed from the plane by his aide. A tall gangling wingless wonder Pilot Officer of youthful appearance, who must have weighed eight stone, if wet. The AOC then uttered the following order to his aide, 'chuck us my sword'. There followed what can only be described as a comedy double act as the AOC adorned himself with his sword and tripped over it as he walked to his car. After witnessing the performance with the sword the need for the car as the final means of transport was obvious.

On another occasion when this AOC visited Abingdon he displayed a human side that made me see him in a different light. His visit was to address the station personnel on a matter of importance. As you can imagine the few, very few members of the station's administration team who had a liking of the bull side of the service decided that this visit would be a good excuse to have a station parade. The parade was duly organised by the few. The AOC arrived and took up his position on the rostrum, a high rostrum due to the AOC's lack of height. He made it clear that he wished us all to hear him clearly and we should break ranks and gather round him. When he finished his address, various senior NCOs attempted to get those present into some sort of parade order. The AOC assessed the situation, uttered the words 'what a ruddy shambles, I'll sort it out'. He then shouted out the order 'parade dismiss'. At that moment the short rotund man whom I had previously looked on as a figure of fun took on the guise of a giant of a man as a result of his quick logical decision and command. I recognised why he was high enough in the pecking order to have a double row of scrambled egg on his hat. A gentleman indeed.

One of the major routine tasks carried out by engine mechanics was refuelling. It is fair to say that this particular operation was the subject of a very strict practice due to the hazardous nature of the job. This was understandable as it was quite normal to fuel an aircraft at the rate of up to fifty gallons of 110 octane Avgas per minute through open ended nozzles. All went well until a French Air Force plane arrived, complete with mechanic. This was just before the 1956 Suez campaign in which we co-operated with the French. The joint campaign was basically to secure international free use of the Suez canal by the shipping of all nations. I have maybe over simplified the situation, but quite frankly I have never had much time for politics or the people who practice them. But back to the French aircraft and its demented mechanic. The aircraft was to be with us for a day or two for tests to be carried out in order to establish a common code of practice and equipment so that British and French paratroop could use the aircraft of either nation. The French mechanic down to his under size black beret and drooping moustache, was the epitome of an apache dancer. He was an affable sort of guy, but we later realised that he was oblivious to the danger and a total menace when it came to the personal safety of himself and those around him. This became obvious when he refuelled his plane. He stood on the wing directly above an open fuel tank and whilst the gasoline was flowing at a fast rate, lit a ruddy great French cigarette. God must have loved this Frenchman, we certainly didn't. We heaved a big sigh of relief when he and his aircraft went back across the channel to France. Hoorah for that bit of water between us and them and blow the channel tunnel.

DH

DE HAVILLAND PROPELLERS LIMITED

School of Propeller Instruction, Worsley Road, Walkden, Lancs.

This is to certify that

2763143 - L.A.C. E.W. Russell.

has successfully completed a five *days*

course of instruction on the types of

DE HAVILLAND PROPELLERS

and ancillary equipment

undermentioned

4 Blade High and Low

Pressure Barrel Type

Propellers

Constant Speed Units

and

Ancillary Equipment.

Course completed 27th April 1956.

[signature] MANAGER

Form No. 2092A/N855A/5.55/B.P. K8416

Chapter 23

ABINGDON MISCELLANY

Being an operational base, RAF Abingdon was an extremely busy airfield. There was always so much happening, personnel never had the time to be bored. Some of the activities involved me directly, others involved me minimally or to such a minor degree, that I had purely a scant knowledge of them. This chapter is a miscellany of items I feel worthy of mention, albeit very briefly. Although I am being brief to the point of vagueness with some of the items in this chapter, I in no way would seek to undermine the importance of any of the functions thus covered, but to make it clear that lack of personal knowledge would not allow me to do differently.

The Parachute School

Although RAF Abingdon was an integral part of transport command, with a heavy demand on its aircraft to fulfil all the world wide commitments that this entailed. There was a further demand to meet the requirements of the parachute training school. This unit was manned by RAF Instructors, who had the task of training mainly parachute regiment personnel to the standard required for them to obtain their wings and cherished red beret. Several of my colleagues volunteered to do the two week course. I readily admit that I didn't volunteer, although I had to wear a parachute on many occasions, the prospect of having to use it left me scared. I never experienced any fear of flying, even inverted flight during aerobatics;

but the thought of jumping out of an aircraft from choice – Ugh. I do however admit to a few, (a very few) moments of regret in later life that I never made a parachute jump one of my achievements. But back to the parachute school. During the two week course which started with ground work in a mockup aircraft, trainees progressed to cable controlled jumpers from a tower onto a jump from a tethered barrage balloon. Next came aircraft familiarisation flights in full kit. The training culminated with a jump from an aircraft, usually over West on the Green. At times the flight would provide an aircraft for more advanced parachutists (Commandos or SAS) to make a water descent into Poole harbour.

THE BALLOON UNIT

This units activities were allied to the parachute school. The unit's basic equipment was a barrage balloon of the type that I well remembered as they were a familiar sight during my growing up in Birmingham during the air raids of the 1940s. Suspended under the balloon was a gondola, that bore a strong resemblance to the body of a personnel carrying military truck. Trainee parachutists would make their first jump from this gondola when it was at a predetermined height from the ground. The height was controlled as the balloon was tethered to a winch by means of a variable length cable. I personally had very little contact with this unit as it operated from an isolated corner of the airfield. I did however meet many members of the unit over numerous glasses of ale in local pubs.

BATTLE OF BRITAIN DAY 1956

I have chosen to deal with this subject in this chapter, as RAF Abingdon did not hold an open day to commemorate the Battle of Britain during my time at the base. I am however aware that the base was open to the public in later years.

In 1956, 1312 flight provided a Hastings aircraft to overfly several bases that would be holding open days. It was decided that the aircraft to be used would be fitted with bomb racks. The racks were to be armed with supply canisters, which would be dropped by parachute over the final airfield that would be overflown. I flew with the aircraft and to be frank our Captain did us proud. When we got to our final airfield he made one overhead pass at about one thousand feet. On the second circuit he dropped the canisters, which I was told looked most impressive from the ground as the assorted coloured parachutes opened. Next the Captain cut two engines, feathered their props and did a low level beat up over the runway. When we landed to retrieve our canisters it was to many remarks of admiration from the visitors who crowded round our aircraft. It was certainly a most memorable afternoon out, and a fitting tribute to a special day.

VISITING AIRCRAFT

I saw many different aircraft as they made brief calls to Abingdon. I even worked on some of them, if I happened to be a member of the duty crew when they visited. Some of the visiting aircraft were mediocre, others were of types that had 'character' and pedigrees that will always promote discussion among those of us who appreciate design and engineering qualities. I recall a clapped out old York that was operated by a civil company that carried freight for the services. This particular aircraft took off side wind so that it could have the benefit of using the longest runway to get off the ground. The York aircraft had done wonderful work a few years earlier during the Berlin air lift. I must admit that even this solitary very tired example looked good as it turned away after takeoff.

On one occasion a Mosquito arrived, this was obviously prearranged; as it remained with us for a few days. During the days it became Groupie's exclusive 'toy'. On the occasions he flew this aircraft he gave one of the finest aerobatics and combat style flying displays that I have ever witnessed. At the completion of each flight he climbed from the cockpit with a look on his face of a man who was totally satisfied with what he had just done. One of our hangars became home to a VIP Hastings for a few days. It was cosmetically different to the normal Hastings as it was luxuriously appointed internally. Its function would normally be to carry Government Ministers, Civil Servants and persons at the lower end of the pecking order during overseas royal visits. I thought then and still do, that it seemed unjust that these parasites and hangers on got far superior travel facilities than service personnel or their families. Two Harvards arrived on one occasion to do some photographic work. The main feature of these aircraft was their similarity of appearance to the Japanese Zeros that had been flown by the Kamikaze Pilots of World War Two.

Many more aircraft visited, but I have chosen just to highlight a few to illustrate how varied a mechanic's day to day working life could be.

AIRCRAFT DEICING

This was without a doubt the most miserable job that could be inflicted on any airman. It was made even worse as it was usually carried out before dawn in the foulest of winter weather. The operation was even worse when it snowed as it was necessary to sweep the snow off the aircraft before the deicing was commenced. Now I'm retired, I find it hard to imagine the way I used to walk on snow covered and icy aircraft wings some thirty-plus-years ago. The actual deicing fluid was a foul, sticky, alcohol based liquid which was supplied in five gallon drums. This foul liquid had to be poured from its drums into a large dispensing tank which was mounted on wheels to give it mobility. This mobility was achieved by airman power, obviously as this was cheaper and more readily available than a tow tractor. The actual deicing process necessitated spraying the wings and tail of the aircraft, in fact all external parts that were particularly vulnerable to icing up. The actual spray nozzles were attached to the end of long tubular hand held wands, which in turn were attached to the fluid container by long flexible hoses. In spite of the operator wearing protective clothing, complete with hood, a fair amount of the foul liquid still got on the person. Not a good way to start the day, particularly even before the luxury of breakfast.

TOOL CHECKS

I of course refer to the ones of a person's trade, not the ones associated with an FFI.

The tool check was an important aspect of service life. Not only was it vital for tradesmen to have a full complement of the correct tools. It was equally important that tools should not get lost or misplaced in areas in which they could create a hazard to people and equipment. It was always necessary to be extra careful when working in the vicinity of aircraft control systems, as a carelessly mislayed tool could have fatal consequences.

I've included this particular subject as I consider the unsophisticated, yet efficient method of checking to be one of the best examples of improvisation that I have ever encountered.

A complete set of tools had been laid out on the large plywood sheet. Next the board and tools had been sprayed over with bright blue paint. When the paint was dry the tools have been removed, leaving the shape of every tool as an area of bare wood. So to check a man's tools he was made to lay them on the board over the appropriate silhouettes, when the layout was complete any deficiency of tools would show up as an area of bare wood.

CREW ROOM AND TEA SWINDLE

The crew room of 1312 flight was a small outbuilding attached to the flights hangar. It was basically used as a place for flight personnel to have a break, a warm in winter, a quick fag or a general skive out of sight of Chiefie. One day per week it became a place of monumental importance when it was used for pay parade. With the unofficial blessing of those in charge we used part of the room to operate a highly organised and profitable tea swindle. Some enterprising airman obtained a 'gash' aircraft water boiler. This was set up and made operative in a discreet corner of the room, well away from the door and prying eyes. Tea, coffee, sugar and milk were purchased at attractive prices from the NAAFI shop. The result was that tea was provided at a nominal price to flight personnel. The facility was also extended to visiting aircrew who would make a generous donation in the tin that was conveniently placed by the tea pot and cups. The profits from this enterprise provided an occasional informal night out for the flight's ground crew. These nights out usually consisted of a gathering in the private back room of a country pub. With of course the provision of food, a piano and a barrel of beer to lubricate the vocal chords. As there was an abundance of pubs in the area of the drome, it was possible to alternate them so as not to wear out our welcome.

GROUND EQUIPMENT

The ground equipment of any flight or squadron was as important to successful servicing and handling of aircraft, as were the tools of each individual tradesman. The ground equipment for 1312 was confined to a section of the flight's hangar. This was when it was not deployed around aircraft. The equipment ranged from a humble wheel chock to complicated generators which were powered by their own vee eight engines. As an engine mechanic I had to do my share of maintenance of this equipment. This involved the daily examination and testing of mechanical plant, replacement of wheels on all manner of hardware ranging from small portable steps to adjustable scaffolding towers. In the case of the old style wooden chocks, part of the maintenance would have been more suited to an old time sailor than an aero engine mechanic. The task in question was the replacement of worn or broken chock ropes, the rope had to be replaced with a piece of half inch sisal, finished to a length of two fathoms with a six to eight inch back splice at both ends. I must admit that I much preferred the later model metal chocks with a chain for pulling them clear. I have little doubt that the efficient presentation of ground equipment was often achieved in the good old and well proven service method of covering it with gallons of paint. In this case sky blue as an alternative to normal white.

AIRCRAFT CLEANING

This was yet another unpleasant job. It was however a very necessary job as not only did the RAF. demand the highest degree of aircraft efficiency, it also demanded the highest degree of aircraft cleanliness. The expected standard applied both internally and externally. Unfortunately the exterior cleanliness was normally achieved as a result of the personal discomfort of airmen like me. Large transport planes would be washed down with large quantities of detergent and water. This was followed with the use of an assortment of sponges, mops, brooms and sweated labour of many hands. Being an engine wallah I normally had the task of cleaning the engine nacelles. They got really filthy, particularly with encrusted carbon and oil deposits in the area of the exhaust outlets. In the case of the Hercules engines, each one had fourteen exhausts. Normally the only way to shift the black carbon deposits was by dipping wire wool in paraffin and then vigorous use of elbow grease. To clean the lower parts of the engine it was necessary to stand on the top of six foot steps. The top of the engine could be done by sitting or kneeling on the front of the wing. It was unfortunate if whilst an airman was cleaning the lower part of an engine, one of his colleagues prematurely cleaned the wing and swept water over the edge. A cry of 'please be careful', or similar, would be heard.

SOCIAL LIFE

The social side of RAF life, for ground crew at least, was very unsophisticated. I have already mentioned the station cinema and the occasional nights out which were associated with the tea swindle profits.

The weekly recreational afternoon was largely a social occasion and was enjoyed by most. Some chose to pursue organised sports, some went for a ramble or cross country run. In the summer months, (weather permitting) many gathered in the meadows along the bank of the river Thames and enjoyed pastimes such as fishing, boating, swimming or just relaxing and enjoying the fresh air. At times I would hitch-hike home and spend a few hours with Mary. On one occasion it was decided to have an all ranks night out for flight personnel. The Guild Hall at Abingdon was booked for the event. This was a particularly fine architecturally attractive old building which had interior walls that were adorned with a fine collection of oil paintings. There was to a live band to provide music for dancing and catering staff from the officers' mess would do the catering for the lavish buffet. One of my colleagues who lived in quarters with his wife and family kindly offered overnight hospitality so that Mary could attend the 'do'. The station CO and his wife, as well as the local Town Clerk and his wife accepted invitations to be guests of the flight. Planning was well advanced when the base got the shock of having one of its Beverley aircraft crash on take off. The aircraft was carrying a large number of service personnel and police dogs who were leaving the UK for overseas postings. The aircraft never got off the ground, but careered through the fence at the end of the runway. Unfortunately a number of deaths occurred. There was obviously an air of depression over the base as a result of this tragic accident. It occurred only a couple of weeks before our special function. It was the feeling of flight members that the event should be cancelled. However, the CO took a hand and said whilst it would not be possible for him to attend, in the interests of flight morale he saw no sensible reason to cancel, particularly as so many of the flight's personnel had played an active part in the preplanning of the function. On the Friday of the function, Mary travelled to Oxford by train. A friend from the flight who was the owner of a rather grand MG saloon car provided the transport from the station, for which I had to reward him with a two gallon petrol coupon. The evening went well, no doubt part of its success was the informality which allowed all ranks to 'mingle' in a very relaxed and congenial atmosphere. One of, if not the most important factor of an airman's (particularly National Service airmans) social life in the 1950s, was that it should not cost much money. During the winter, in the company of a few friends I spent many evenings in the local pubs, there were many within walking distance of the drome. Not for us the consuming of endless pints of ale. Apart from not being able to afford to do this, the local brew in my opinion was weak and foul tasting. The main objective of these evenings was a game of darts with some congenial company, particularly in a warm bar with an open fire. Evenings of this kind could be had for a short brisk walk and the price of two or three half pints.

End of Abingdon miscellany.

Chapter 24

ROUTE FLYING

This was a prime function of transport command. In the case of 1312, route flying was not carried out as frequently as with other squadrons and flights. This was as a result of the major commitment of the provision of aircraft for paratroop and supply drop training that was a major part of the transport supply function. On the brief occasions when 1312 provided an aircraft for a route trip, provided it was not a personnel carrying flight, an engine and airframe fitter would normally travel on the aircraft. To give an example of what a route flight was all about, I have chosen to describe one that I flew on. The one I describe is typical of the hundreds of similar journeys of the 1950s. This was a period which saw British service personnel, (very often with their families) manning bases all over the World. These varied in size from small staging posts and jungle outposts to huge bases that resembled mini towns. It befell transport command to constantly move vast amounts of personnel and freight to ensure the smooth operation of these bases. The journey I describe was made by Handley Page Hastings. Similar flights were also made by Valettas, as the latter was a two engined aircraft with a smaller fuel capacity than the Hastings, its individual stages tended to be shorter, it was often convenient to make the overnight stops at major refuelling stops. The plan for the trip I have chosen to describe was for the plane to be flown to RAF Lyneham, where it would be loaded for the journey. For this trip the plane was to be in freight carrying role, although six passenger seats would be carried to allow for the unknown. It was necessary to go to Lyneham to collect freight as

Abingdon did not have a bulk freight facility, it did develop one at a later stage when two of the resident squadrons converted to Beverleys.

The main item of freight was to be a replacement engine for an aircraft that was US and AOG at Habbiniya in Iraq. It would be necessary to refuel at Luqa, Malta. The return route from Iraq was to be via North Africa, which would enable us to service two more British bases. Namely El Adem (inland from Tobruk) and Castel Beneto, (Idris) in Libya. This particular trip had the advantage of being a weekday consignment, so I would not sacrifice a treasured weekend at home.

The crew consisted of a Flight Lieutenant as first dicky and Captain, a Pilot Officer as second dicky. The other crew members - navigator, radio operator and flight engineer were either Sergeants or Flight Sergeants. There was no AQM as it was not a passenger flight. My colleague and I would act as freight checkers and tea makers during the flight. The schedule of operation was as follows.

First Day

A morning spent in putting the aircraft into freight role and getting all service documentation in order for being absent from home base and the UK. After lunch we departed from Abingdon for the short flight to RAF Lyneham, where the aircraft was to be loaded. The aircraft was handed over to the freight section, this completed, our work for the day was all over. Our quarters for the night were to be at the Lyneham transit camp. This was a coach ride from the base at a place called Clyffe Pypard. This particular transit camp was typical of a military establishment of yesteryear. It was located on the top of an inhospitable windy ridge and consisted of a collection of aged wooden billets. Thank goodness it was only to be my home for one night. I thought I'd finished with accommodation of this type when I departed from RAF Weeton. In spite of its somewhat primitive appearance, the accommodation was warm and comfortable, the orderly even put a hot water bottle in my bed, what luxury. The air frame fitter and I shared a billet as we didn't qualify for the same mess accommodation as the air crew. We retired early as it was necessary to rise at 5.00 a.m. the following day.

Second Day

We responded to our early call; washed, shaved, breakfasted and gathered at 6.00 a.m. for the transport to Lyneham. On arrival the air crew went to flight control to collect an assortment of documents, including maps and flight instructions. Whilst this was going on my colleague and I drew rations for the day, checked the aircraft fuel state and the security of the freight which had been loaded overnight. The load was secured to the aircraft floor by means of chains and adjustable turnbuckles. The crew arrived and we were in the air by about 8.00 a.m. It was a routine, uneventful flight, we landed at Luqa mid afternoon, in weather that was much warmer than that we had left in the UK.

The transit hotel at Luqa was far superior to Clyffe Pypard. Luqa was a major stop over for service personnel and families as they moved to or from the UK to take up postings. My companion and I were allocated a room for our one night stop. We showered, changed into civilian clothes and enjoyed a good meal in the mess. It was then time to enjoy a few hours' recreation. We decided to go and have a look at Valetta, which was only a short bus ride from Luqa. To those who have never had the experience of a bus ride in Malta, it can only be described as an experience. An experience that puts the bus drivers of British Cities amongst the elite of their profession. It only remains to say that particular bus ride was without a doubt the hairiest I have ever made. I found Valetta a fascinating City. One could not help but get a feel for its historic and often violent past. In the mid fifties it still bore the signs of its suffering during the Second World War. Some parts still had debris that had not been cleared from that time. We spent a pleasant evening looking at the sights, including Straight Street, (only looking). I will admit to having a beer in one of the many bars in that Street. We finished our evening with a meal at the services club. We decided to invest a modest sum in a taxi ride back to Luqa as it would have been a pity to spoil what had been a pleasant evening with another ride on a Maltese bus. The following day was to be another fairly early start. This was necessary as we would be flying towards the heat of the East and our aircraft was not pressurised and air conditioned. Hooray for the proper aviating of yesteryear.

Third Day

Another early start. No matter, I was used to them. Before I became an airman I used to set out out from home on my bicycle at 6.40 a.m. to be at work by 7.30 a.m. So early starts never troubled me, but they would now. Some of the freight had been removed over night and replaced with items to be taken on to our other refuelling and night stops. The day's flying was along the Mediterranean, passing Crete and Cyprus. We crossed the coast and seemed to fly over endless desert, with the occasional sighting of an oasis or small settlement. There was one feature in this boring landscape which was not only spectacular in its appearance, but acted as a useful day time navigational aid. This feature was the Great Lebanon. A huge mountain that not only broke up the endless desert landscape, it had the appearance of a monumental iced cake with its snowcapped peak. It was indeed a truly wondrous sight. In the early afternoon on the distant horizon we saw two long twisting lines across the desert. These lines marked the courses of the Tigres and Euphrates rivers which was a sign that it was time to commence our descent for landing at Habbaniya. Our instructions were to land at the plateau air strip, this landing area was a short distance from the main base, but was often used for transport planes. When the landing was complete the plane was taxied to a dispersal and parked as directly by the ground crew. The door was opened and before we had time to disembark a crowd of Iraqi labour swarmed in with the express purpose of having a scavenge in our ration boxes to see if we had left any food. Before we left the dispersal local female labourers in RAF employment put steps up to each engine and wiped away any traces of oil to prevent sand settling on it. The Captain handed the aircraft over to the ground crew and we boarded the bus for the short ride to the main base. This base was so vast that it had an internal taxi service. The transit accommodation was primitive, it was in fact a square bell tent with a sand floor. A camp bed was provided, with a substantial supply of blankets. Those who have ever slept on a camp bed will be aware of the amount of cold that strikes up from below, this was particularly so in the desert, hence the large number of blankets.

The food in the transit mess came in tins and was fortunately of UK origin. I must admit that my tinned steak was good. During the hours of daylight it was far too hot to perspire and one felt dehydrated. As I was only there for a short time it was possible to overcome the problem with iced beer, that's my excuse. The NAAFI had not only a good supply of beer, but also black and white brand cigarettes in tins of twenty at 1/6 (7 ½p) per tin. I was fortunate indeed in only being at Habbaniya for one night. I could not have stood being posted to such an inhospitable dump.

Fourth Day

We departed from Habbaniya for the return flight to the UK with a passenger. Not a human passenger, a four legged passenger. To be precise, a ruddy huge black Labrador dog that spent the entire remaining two days of the trip in being air sick. Ugh. This situation came about as the result of a high ranking officer, who on completion of his tour of duty, decided to drive back to the UK. He was high enough in the pecking order to decree that his dog be flown back to quarantine in the UK to avoid complications at the many frontiers he would cross during his return by road. It was also financially sensible from his point of view to send his dog on an RAF flight at tax payers expense. So that is the circumstances of how we got lumbered with a smelly dog for two days in the confines of an aeroplane. Most of the day's flying was over desert, with the exception of a small part of the Eastern Mediterranean. It was possible when flying at twenty thousand feet over the North African desert to pick out many features on the ground. I clearly saw many irregular shaped areas of PSP which no doubt were the remains of World War Two air strips and military installations. It was also possible to see the occasional bit of long abandoned military hardware.

This was the longest leg of the flight and it would be necessary to make a brief refuelling stop before the overnight stop of Castel Beneto was reached. In mid afternoon we made our refuelling stop at El Adem, a British manned base a few miles inland from Tobruk. The place can best be described as dusty and hot. Its endearing features were the chance to have a pee in a proper toilet, a quick meal sitting at a table and of course several bottles of ice cold beer from the fridge. I was easily pleased, in fact I still am. After a break of about one hour we were again on our way for the short flight to Castel Beneto. This place was so different from the previous night's stop at Habbaniya. The accommodation at Castel Beneto resembled a North African Hotel as depicted in Hollywood films of the time. My companion and I were shown to a room that led off a large palm shaded courtyard. I managed a brief look around the base before darkness fell. The base was guarded and patrolled by locally recruited RAF Regiment personnel. I made a brief unofficial call at a stall in the regiment's accommodation compound and obtained a couple of kilos of new potatoes to take home. The evening was spent in the bar, this was a rather grand place. I was able to buy a couple of bottles of good vintage port at 2/6 (12 ½p) per bottle. There was a party of fairly new airmen in the bar, spending the evening getting drunk. It was their first night away from the UK enroute to postings in Aden. In my opinion they had good cause to get drunk, in their position most airmen would have done the same. A feature worthy of mention was the barman at Castel Beneto. He was an Italian and had commenced his employment when it was an Italian outpost. Along came the Germans and kicked the Italians out, the barman remained. Later the British arrived on the scene and booted the Germans out; the barman still remained behind his bar, no doubt doing very well.

Fifth Day

I woke after a good night's sleep. That is not totally true. No problem about the good night's sleep bit, but I was in fact woken up. I was woken by a nudge on the shoulder and a voice saying 'cup of tea Johnny'. I had no cause to complain as it was an Arab orderly offering me tea in bed, the only tea I ever had in bed during my RAF service. I'm sure you will agree this makes it worthy of mention. We took off for home, complete with our now very smelly canine passenger, plus a full load of miscellaneous freight we had gathered during our travels. The days flight was routine and of about six hour's duration. We touched down in mid afternoon at RAF Northolt. This was necessary so that the dog could be collected by the Quarantine Authorities and the aircraft and crew could be seen by UK Customs. The customs was purely routine, except that the Officer showed interest in a gold Avia watch I was wearing. I was however able to satisfy him that I had not obtained it outside the UK, it was a much treasured possession that my wife had bought for my twenty first birthday.

When all the formalities had been dealt with, the plan was to fly back to Abingdon via Lyneham. As it was now the weekend, I was given permission to proceed home from Northolt. So I set off complete with my cheap fags, two kilos of spuds, two bottles of port plus an assortment of miscellaneous souvenirs to hitchhike home.

What I have described is typical of a short route flight of that period. Even after almost forty years I still have one item to remind me of the flight. The item is a Maltese lace tablecloth which was a very fine example of a George Cross in its pattern.

Luxury Transit Hotel RAF Idris (Castel Benito) Libya 1956

Transit Hotel – Luqa (Malta) 1956

Transit 'Billet' bedouin style RAF Habbaniya (Iraq) 1956

Chapter 25

EPILOGUE

As I progressed with the writing of this tale, I often thought that I would not reach this stage. But reach it I have, so let's write a final 'ruddy good show'.

I said at the beginning that my story would be loosely based on my experiences and observations of National Service. It must be obvious to my readers that I have used a certain amount of artist's license and done a bit of line shooting. But how much? I'm not saying, so you must draw your own conclusion. During the writing of this book, I realised how fortunate my generation had been by having such a lesson of life (National Service) forced upon us. Particularly as it occurred at an age that allowed us to learn from the experience. It obviously didn't appear that way as we left our homes and civilian employment to join up. Many of us were married men with home and family responsibilities. Some of my generation did not do National Service. To those who missed it due to being medically unfit I offer my understanding and sympathy. To those who missed it due to their strong personal convictions, provided they did some work for the benefit of their fellow beings, I offer my sincere admiration, for the courage they showed. But to those who dodged National Service for selfish reasons, particularly the ones who carried on to fame and fortune whilst others served, I offer nothing but utter comtempt.

National Service is now dead and buried and has been for many years. We now have the benefit of a totally professional and career based mixture of armed services which is made up of men and women of whom we can be justly proud. I don't think any right thinking person would like to return to the days of young people being compelled to become members of a service in which they had no desire to serve.

However, I do feel we need some sort of National Organisation to encourage a sense of self discipline into young people during their impressionable years. Who knows the answer?

I certainly don't.

Cardington from the air

Chapter 26

APPENDIX ONE

RAF CARDINGTON

An abridged version of the history of the above establishment which was kindly provided by the CO in August 1993.

In 1917 the land of Cardington was purchased by the Royal Navy for the construction of an airship works. Short Brothers developed the works and constructed the R31 and R32 in a giant double bay hangar which was seven hundred foot and cost £110,000=.

The Air Ministry took over in 1919. It was renamed the Royal Airship Works in 1921. In 1926/27 the airship shed was enlarged to eight hundred and twelve feet long, two hundred and seventy-five feet wide and one hundred and eighty feet high to take the R101.

Over the following years the base was put to many uses, such as aircraft storage, restoration of historic aircraft, training of barrage balloon operators, recruit training and a demobilisation base.

The base still functions as an RAF maintenance unit, but enjoys a multi purpose role as a home to several other Government controlled functions.

The aerial photograph was taken in 1991 and clearly shows the line of the railway I travelled along. No doubt the track disappeared during the Beeching era, also clearly visible is the airship shed and outline of the old airfield.

Gate Guardian at Bridgnorth. This guardian posed less of a threat to recruits than did the 'Human' variety.

Chapter 27

APPENDIX TWO

ROYAL AIR FORCE BRIDGNORTH

The following is a brief history of the above establishment. It has been compiled from information which has kindly been provided by members of the Bridgnorth branch of the RAFA.

RAF Bridgnorth, (known locally as RAF Stanmore), functioned from 1939 until its closure in 1963. It was then returned to agricultural use with part of the site becoming an industrial estate. Shropshire County Council have carried out considerable landscaping work on the road side of the site and there is little doubt that as time progresses this will mature into a very attractive aspect. It is intended that a permanent memorial will be established to the many ex RAF personnel who trained there. The establishment trained many thousands of personnel, not only from Britain but from many European and Commonwealth lands. The memorial will be located in the area of the old original boiler house and will serve as a fitting reminder of the important start that the station gave many RAF personnel at the beginning of their service.

I am indebted to John Mahon for the loan of photographs of RAF Bridgnorth from his private collection.

Row of billets at RAF Bridgnorth. Typical of those to be seen in bases of all three branches of the services during the 1940's & 50's.

Chapter 28

APPENDIX THREE

ROYAL AIRFORCE WEETON

Brief history of RAF Weeton compiled from information given by a member of RAFA. Preston branch. The gentleman in question was able to speak with good authority as during his service career he twice served at Weeton for a total of approximately eight years.

RAF Weeton was conceived in 1938. It opened its gates to the driving school in 1939. Over the years the station had four wings, these being largely devoted to the training of technical subjects. The courses covered ranged in duration from six weeks to two years. During the 1950s there was even a recruit training section. The base was vacated by the RAF during the 1960s. The hospital has long gone, together with the hutted accommodation. Considerable development has taken place over recent years with the construction of brick built barracks, which are now occupied by the army.

NOTICE OF ENLISTMENT IN CLASS H OF THE R.A.F. RESERVE

You, No. 2763143 .... Rank .... S.A.C. .... Name .... Russell E.W. ....

are hereby notified that you have been deemed to be enlisted in Class H of the R.A.F. Reserve to undergo part-time service, for which you are liable under the National Service Acts, 1948, with effect from ...... 12th August, 1957 ...

The Reserve Centre to which you are allocated is :—

No. .... R.A.F. Reserve Centre,

Address ....

....

....

UNIT DATE STAMP
17 JUL 1957
Signature of Airman
E W Russell

Remobilisation Station ....

Signed .... [signature] ....

Rank .... Flight Lieutenant, ...

Commanding .... R.A.F. Abingdon ....

WARNING

(To the airman/~~airwoman~~ named on this Form)

(i) You are hereby reminded that the unauthorised communication by you to another person at any time of any information you may have acquired whilst in Her Majesty's Service which might be useful to an enemy in war renders you liable to prosecution under the Official Secrets Act.

(ii) Your discharge does not remove any liability you may still have to be called up for further national service or any such liability that may be placed upon you by future legislation.

(iii) You should on no account part with this certificate or forward it by post when applying for a situation, but should use a copy attested by a responsible person. If the certificate is lost it will be replaced only when its loss can be proved to have been due to very exceptional circumstances. Application for replacement should be made to the Air Officer Commanding, Royal Air Force Record Office, Gloucester.

ANY PERSON finding this Certificate is requested to forward it in an unstamped envelope to the Under Secretary of State, Air Ministry, London, W.C.2.

Chapter 29

APPENDIX FOUR

ROYAL AIRFORCE ABINGDON ON THAMES

The station started its life in 1932. It was the home of many different squadrons prior to the Second World War. During the war it was responsible for the training of a considerable number of aircrew members on Whitley bombers. It also had the distinction of providing bombers and crews to take part in some of the first thousand bomber raids on Cologne, Essen and other Cities in Germany. After the war the base was destined to become one of the major dromes associated with the Berlin air lift. When I was posted to Abingdon in 1956 it was the home base to numbers 24 and 47 squadrons, which at that time operated Hastings aircraft. In addition to these it was also home to 1312 TSF, (my outfit) which operated both Hastings and Valetta aircraft. Number one parachute training school was also in residence. As well as the Hastings and Valettas the base had a small flight of Chipmunks which 1312 personnel maintained. The final resident aircraft was a rather ancient Tiger Moth which belonged to the flying club of one of the squadrons. During my time at Abingdon, (1956/57) numbers 24 and 47 squadrons converted to the huge Blackburn Beverley freighters. At about the same time 1312 TSF became TSE, but carried on functioning as before. The station continued to function in many different operational roles for several years. In the early

1990s the base was vacated by the RAF At the time of writing this, (late 1993) the army are in occupation and the base is now known as Dalton barracks.

RUDDY POOR SHOW.

Picture of Vickers Valetta

Copy of information pamphlet that was issued to service personnel who found themselves at RAF Luqa during the 1950's. Whether there as a result of a permanent posting or transit.

"MALTA GEN"

ROYAL AIR FORCE

ROYAL AIR FORCE LUQA

Distance from London — 1307 miles.
Time difference from G.M.T. — Plus 1 hour.

INFORMATION FOR PASSENGERS

Malta is a small rocky island, roughly $\frac{2}{3}$ rds the size of the Isle of Wight, situated almost half way between Gibraltar and the Canal Zone. It has always been considered of considerable strategic importance and in consequence, its history records a great deal of strife. Valletta, the capital city contains many reminders of the past which are well worth seeing.

Your stay on the island may be short, but we hope that it will be interesting and comfortable.

You will be notified of the time of departure of the aircraft on the notice board in your mess. Night-stopping passengers are given an early call *Two Hours* before take-off, and are picked up by coach *One Hour* before take-off.

All airmen in transit over 24 hours must report to the Transit Orderly Room in the Transit Mess before leaving the camp.

AIR BOOKING CENTRE. If you have to change into another aircraft, or hold papers for your return journey, you must contact the A.B.C. immediately.

EXCHANGE OF CURRENCY may be effected up to a limited amount, by the Currency Exchange Officers in the Air Booking Centre.

BAGGAGE. It is your responsibility to ensure that your night-stopping kit is returned to the aircraft. *Valuable Items* may be handed to the Officer i/c Transit Mess, for safe custody. Every precaution will be taken to safeguard these items, but they will be accepted only at owner's risk.

MESS FACILITIES are provided for your comfort and for that of the passengers who will follow after you. Please treat the mess with care.

WATER is always a problem on the island, owing to its acute shortage. *Don't waste it.*

ENTRTAINMENTS. Most forms of entertainment are available in Valletta, which is about 3 miles from Luqa. A civilian bus service runs from near the Transit Messes. The last bus back is at 2130 hours daily. Buses hired by P.S.I. Luqa also return from Castile Place, Valletta at 2140, 2200, 2230, 2300 and 2330 hours daily, and transient personnel may make use of them. In addition to Cinemas in Valletta, the Station Cinema gives two performances daily at 1800 and 2000 hours. A bus, to and from the Cinema at a fare of one penny each way, stops outside the Resident Officers' Mess on the main public road.

TAXIS may be hired from outside the Officers' Transit Mess. Information on fares is available in the Mess but you are advised to agree with the driver the amount to be paid before undertaking the journey.

GUIDE BOOKS OF MALTA. For the convenience of passengers, Guide Books are displayed in the respective Transit Hotels.

RAOC/P&SS/10,000/17/3/55.J.1429.